9 FORMULAS

FOR

Competitive

BUSINESS
SUCCESS

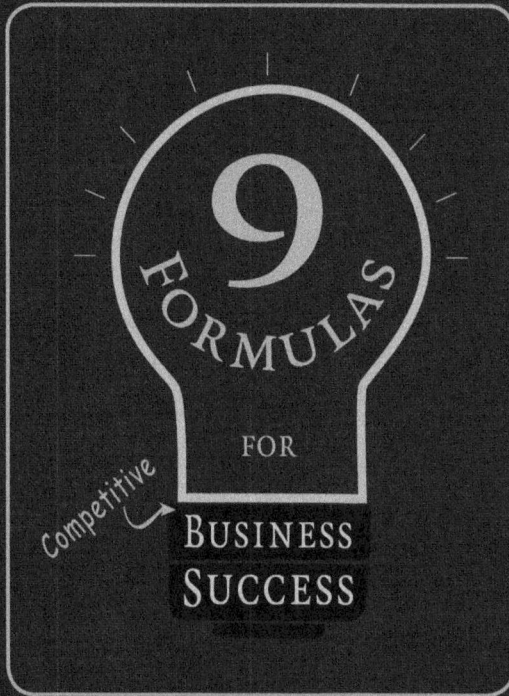

The Science of Strategy

Gary Gagliardi

Winning Consistently

The book explains an easy-to-use strategy for building successful businesses. The author used this system to build his own company, one of the Inc. 500 fastest growing companies in America. The system itself, however, is much older, based on Sun Tzu's competitive principles that have been handed down and practiced for 2,500 years.

The nine formulas in this book describe a process of building up competitive positions and advancing them. It starts with collecting the right information. Then learning how to spot opportunities and analyzing them which ones you are best positioned to use. It teaches you how to minimize risks when you committing to a move and how to foresee and respond to the nine situations you are likely to encounter. As you move forward, it teaches you how to use your position to build momentum, maximize your rewards, and protect what you have built.

The nine formulas in the book are presented like recipes, describing the ingredients needed from your environment and how you put those ingredients together to create a successful enterprise. You don't have to be born a genius to understand this competitive strategy. The nine formulas in this book make this process much easier.

This process is based on making simple comparisons. The right comparisons lead to the right decisions. Your decisions determine your competitive position. It is this position that other people compare with the positions of others. It is their decisions that determine whether or not you are successful.

Award Recognition for *Art of War* Strategy Books
by Gary Gagliardi

The Golden Key to Strategy

Psychology/Self-Help
Ben Franklin
Book Award
2006 - Winner

*The Art of War Plus
The Ancient Chinese Revealed*

Multicultural Nonfiction
Independent Publishers
Book Award
2003 - Winner

*Making Money by Speaking:
The Spokesperson Strategy*

Career
Foreword Magazine
Book of the Year
2007 - Finalist

Strategy for Sales Managers

Business
Independent Publishers
Book Award
2006 - Semi-Finalist

*The Warrior Class:
306 Lessons in Strategy*

Self-Help
Foreword Magazine
Book of the Year
2005 - Finalist

Strategy Against Terror

Philosophy
Foreword Magazine
Book of the Year
2005 - Finalist

*The Ancient Bing-fa:
Martial Arts Strategy*

Sports
Foreword Magazine
Book of the Year
2007 - Finalist

*The Art of War
Plus Its Amazing Secrets*

Multicultural Nonfiction
Independent Publishers
Book Award
2005 - Finalist

The Warrior's Apprentice

Youth Nonfiction
Independent Publishers
Book Award
2006 - Semi-Finalist

Published by

Science of Strategy Institute, Clearbridge Publishing

Second Edition

ISBN 978-1-929194-94-0 (1-929194-943)

Copyright 2006, 2015 Gary Gagliardi

Registered with Department of Copyrights, Library of Congress

Publisher's Cataloging-in-Publication Data

 1. Strategy. 2. Philosophy. 3. Business management.
4. New business enterprise—U.
S. 5. Home-based business. I. Gagliardi, Gar y 1951—. II. Nine Formulas for
Business [Competitive] Success
HF5438.5.S86 2006
658.8 /1 21 —dc21

Library of Congress Catalog Card Number: 2006902147

Science of Strategy Institute/Clearbridge Publishing
2829 Linkview Dr. Las Vegas, NV, 89134
Phone: (702) 721-9631
gagliardi.gary@gmail.com
scienceofstrategy.org

Nine Formulas

for Business Success

by Gary Gagliardi

Science of Strategy Institute

Clearbridge Publishing

9 FORMULAS

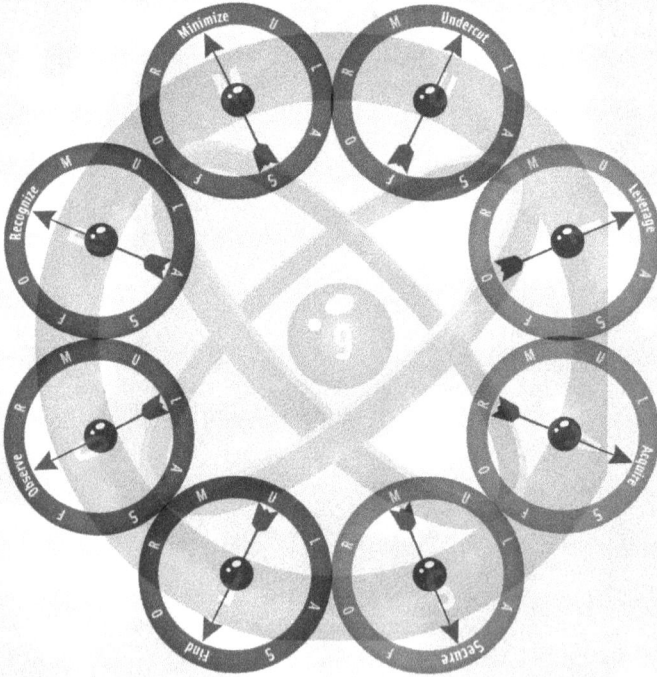

ONE SCIENCE:
The Science of Strategy

Contents

Nine Formulas for Success

About this Book

If it is true that amateurs borrow but geniuses steal, this work must qualify as a work of genius. Almost every paragraph in it is a restatement of concepts that originally appeared 2,500 years ago in Sun Tzu's *The Art of War*.

The larger truth is that almost every concept in modern military and business strategy originally appeared in Sun Tzu's work. Interestingly, much of today's research about how people make decisions is also rediscovering the principles that Sun Tzu explained over two millennia ago. His work was, after all, a work about making better decisions in life and death situations.

Sun Tzu's book was written as a series of scientific formulas. Unfortunately, when translated into English sentences, those formulas sound like vague aphorisms. Scientific formulas are too conceptual to translated easily. In the original Chinese, Sun Tzu's formulas are very abstract. They apply to any form of competition. They are put into the context of military competition in order to make them more easily understood.

In that tradition, I have put those same concepts into the context of business strategy. The goal is to make them easier for today's readers to appreciate. I have authored several dozen books on Sun Tzu's strategic system. Most of them are on business competition. Many of them have been developed out of my work training people from some of the nation's largest organizations.

Most recently, I completed a nine-volume work called ***Sun Tzu's Playbook***, consisting of over two hundred and thirty articles explaining different aspects of Sun Tzu's philosophy in a modern context. Its examples are mostly from business, but also sports, romance, career choices, and so on. This work might be seen as a condensed version of that work, but it was actually the larger works forerunner. The nine volumes of that work are expanded versions of the nine chapters in this work.

This work is like Sun Tzu's book in another way. It offers a lot of ideas in a few number of pages. After reading it, my wife said it was more like nine hundred formulas than nine. This is both a complement and a criticism.

Unlike when this book was first published, almost a decade ago, readers today can delve into any of the topics covered here more deeply in the Playbook articles. The list of related articles follow each chapter. They are available individually as PDFs, interconnection, on-line to Institute members, and in book form (printed and eBook) in the nine volumes of the ***Playbook***.

Gary Gagliardi

—STRATEGY 101—
THE SUCCESS FORMULAS

Know How to Compete

You get nine powerful formulas in this book. Each will bring you a step close to making your dreams come true. Learning them will change your life. Though we discuss these formulas in terms of business success, they can make you more successful in any competitive aspect of your life.

These formulas teach you how to compete. They come from the science of strategy. Like most sciences, strategy is based on methods that can reproduce results consistently. These methods break down the algorithms of strategy into simple steps. Following these formulas is no more complex than baking a cake. By the end of this book, you will understand how to use these formulas and you will understand why they are certain to work.

The Formulas for Success

Why is success easier using these particular formulas?

Success can be simple. You don't have to be perfect. You only have to be better than your competitors. Successful people have one thing in common. They know how to compete. Successful people are not always great business people. Successful enterprises are not always excellent businesses. Both do only one thing very well: outmaneuver their competitors.

Notice that we don't say, "beat their competitors." Among the many things most people don't understand is that success isn't about fighting battles and beating opponents. Fighting is costly, even if you win. Strategy is the science of leveraging situation, especially the mistakes of your competitors, to make yourself successful without fighting costly battles.

The secret of dominating competitors so that they cannot fight you is positioning. You dominate competitors by developing dominating competitive positions. These positions win business in a way that competitors cannot attack.

You cannot leap into a dominating position any more than you can leap to the top of a building. You build a dominating position over time. It is like climbing a ladder, one rung at a time. If you know how to build a competitive position, dominating the competition is easy.

> *Our books on strategy win award recognition every year because the science makes such rare, good sense!*

You will love this book because it makes sense. It makes sense despite the fact that competitive systems don't work the way you think they should. Much of strategy is nonintuitive.

Some of strategy is counterintuitive. A little of it is just plain crazy. Strategy has its own logic, but it works. What more can you ask?

This book gives you a big-picture view of strategy. Once you master it, this viewpoint is breathtaking. This system fits with everything you already know about business, but it explains why a few people are so successful while most are not. This elegant system fills in the blanks in your understanding of business.

The formulas in this book work. In reading through them, you will understand why they work. We wanted to boil the science of strategy down to its simplest elements. Though it encapsulates only a small fraction of the complete science, this book is the best possible introduction to using strategy to make yourself successful.

Remember:

- ✖ Competitive success is different than just doing business.
- ✖ The formulas in this book are the simplest, most complete, and most advanced expression of the science of strategy.

The Formula System

What does this system of strategy entail?

Strategy teaches that people win competitive contests because they have dominant positions. Battles are won by positioning before they are fought. Even better, if you develop a dominant position the smartest competitors won't even try to fight you. Of course, competitors aren't always smart, but you'd rather fight dumb competitors than smart ones, wouldn't you?

Strategy teaches that everyone has a competitive position. In the ongoing journey to bigger and better things, your existing position is just your starting point. The techniques of strategy focus on advancing and building up that position over time. Success isn't an endpoint in this journey. Success is maintaining and expanding your dominance over competitors.

The nine formulas in this book describe how you build dominant positions. Every chapter focuses on a different aspect of your journey. To build a position, you must respond appropriately to an array of competitive situations. We organize, categorize, and explain the issues with which you must deal.

The nine formulas represent the nine steps you take, one after another, to advance your position. These steps are

- comparing your position to competitors' positions,
- building competitive channels of information,
- identifying the best opportunities to advance,
- identifying the restrictions on defending and advancing,
- pursuing new competitive positions safely,
- responding to challenges in building a position,
- creating the momentum to make a position dominating,
- testing the profitability of a new position, and
- defending a new position from competitive attack.

We cover a ton of material here. We want to help you remember the flow of these lessons. To make this easy, we use the acronym 9 FORMULAS. The first letter of each of our formulas spells out 9 FORMULAS. We use alliterative formula names, repeating the key initial, to make our basic lessons easier to remember.

Don't think of the nine formulas as a to-do list. You don't even check them off as accomplished. These nine formulas represent a cycle of activities. The first formula is the core of the cycle. The other eight formulas revolve around it. You simply go through this cycle again and again to advance your position again and again.

Remember:

- ⊗ These nine formulas form a complete system.
- ⊗ This system advances your competitive position.
- ⊗ Success means continually advancing your position.

These Formulas Are Different

How can I know that this book doesn't just rehash everything I've read about business a hundred times before?

Every other business book you've read tells a lot of nice success stories. This book doesn't. Other books offer a few fairly simple, somewhat disconnected ideas about the ingredients of success. This book puts all those ideas into a comprehensive system. Most books seek to inspire. This book seeks to educate. Building a dominating business position is very different than what is taught in most books on business.

So, how do you build up a dominating strategic position?

Our first formula, 9 KEY COMPONENTS, describes the parts that make up a strategic position. It puts your competitive position in a tangible form. The elements that define a position are not vague, subjective, or touchy-feely. These elements are solid and real—as solid as steel, as real as gold. Different people using this system of analysis must come to the exact same conclusions about the relative weaknesses and strengths of you and your competitors.

The process of advancing a position is called the PROGRESS CYCLE. This process is described by the eight other formulas in this book. This process leverages the situations you encounter to improve your competitive position over time. It teaches you how to identify competitive

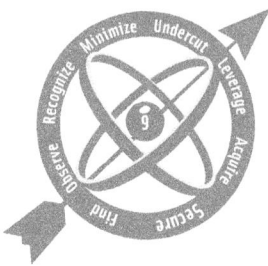

conditions and respond to them appropriately.

The idea behind the Progress Cycle is simple. To advance your position, you must take advantage of opportunities. You do not create opportunities. You can only use the opportunities created by others, mostly by your competitors. To use an opportunity, you must exploit the weaknesses of your competitors. To use it to secure a position, you must overcome a number of challenges. After you have advanced your position, you must know how to defend it.

People are surprised that strategy doesn't focus on defeating competitors as much as on using them.

This book will introduce you to this process for the first time. I could have added a thousand more pages offering examples of all these ideas, but I don't like reading big, thick books and I certainly don't like writing them. These formulas are succinct. They are simply an introduction. The Science of Strategy Institute offers a wealth of other materials that describe these systems in more detail. (*Subliminal message: You will buy more of our books after finishing this one!*)

Remember:

-   We don't tell you stories about other people's success.
-   We give you the steps for writing your own success story.
-   The process makes obvious sense once you know it.

Formulas That Others Miss

Doesn't everyone know what the formulas for competitive success in business are?

Success isn't about management, planning, marketing, sales, or quality. It is about being better than your competitors. You don't have to be better in every respect. You just have to be better at a specific place and time.

Though many people call themselves "strategists," very few people are trained in strategic competition. Most people know a few basic principles of strategy—such as the idea that the best defense is a good offense—but you will rarely find a person who knows the specific conditions under which these principles must be applied.

All businesses have many things in common. They must market, make, sell, and deliver their products and services. In doing these tasks, all businesses try to make a profit. A few of

The most successful people in business are those who know the one thing that always matters: how to win.

them actually do. Despite seemingly having the same functional parts, there is a world of difference between a successful business and most businesses.

Successful people know how to compete. Most business people do not. Eighty percent of new business fail within the first two years. These people aren't stupid. Look at all the talent and money that went into the dot-com boom in the '90s. What happened? They call it the dot-com bust.

How does a successful business find a position that dominates its competition? Some businesses are just lucky. Most are led by people with a special, intuitive sense of how strategy works. Fortunately, you don't have to be born with this rare talent. You don't have to be a genius to master strategy. You can learn strategy. Successful people get into dominant positions by following certain rules. This book tells you those rules.

The most successful business people follow these rules even though most don't know them. Seventy percent of the Fortune 500 disappear every couple of decades. When their well-proven methods go wrong, all their high-priced, experienced professional managers and consultants cannot figure it out and fix it. People can be successful without knowing why. If business schools taught people how to compete, every MBA would be running his or her own successful business. Very few actually do.

Remember:

- For most businesses finding success is like magic.
- Very smart people make very big competitive mistakes.
- Magic formulas can always stop working for "no reason."
- Real formulas work for clear reasons.

Formulas Describe Systems

Don't hundreds of other books describe why some business fail while others succeed?

Few books discuss businesses as complex, competitive systems. Most business books oversimplify the complex environment in which businesses compete. This competitive environment is chaotic and dynamic. Most business gurus reach into the complex cauldron of competition and pull out a few qualities that are sometimes important. This book offers a different vision of competitive systems.

All systems are more than the sum of their parts. To compete, a business must be complete. If a single key part is missing, the quality of its other parts doesn't matter. Success comes from the interaction of the parts more than from the quality of the parts.

The formulas in this book describe businesses as systems functioning within the larger systems of the business environment. Strategy is the study of competitive systems. Every formula in this book describes system interactions—how doing one thing affects other aspects of the system.

The science of strategy focuses on the critical issues of survival. Strategy analyzes how a given enterprise can compete more successfully under a range of changing conditions. It seeks to understand how competitors react to opportunities and challenges, how actions create responses, and how certain actions lead to success. Strategy looks at the overall fitness of a system to compete.

There is a science to winning, a science that most people do not know exists.

The nine formulas of strategy are simple ways of describing competitive fitness. These formulas describe what actions you need to take and how they affect the system. These formulas are precise ways of describing the interactions of relationships in the marketplace. Using these formulas, you learn to see your business in a new and more powerful way.

Remember:

- If you are missing a key ingredient, you aren't competitive.
- Businesses must be seen as whole systems.
- Strategy is the study of competitive systems.
- Formulas define how parts work in a system.

Formulas for Survival

If business schools aren't teaching these formulas for success, where do they come from?

There are tens of thousands of successful companies in the world. Most of these businesses compete well because their leader has an intuitive sense for systems. Their individual success, however, isn't a generic recipe that you can follow. Most successful business leaders are like master chefs. They know from feel and experience what works and doesn't work. They don't work from recipes. Their sense for systems allows them to improvise. This makes for great stories but not for useful formulas you can use.

The formulas in this book are different. They describe competitive systems in a timeless, universal way. They can be applied to any business in any industry at any time.

Powerful natural dynamics underlie all human competition. Physical, psychological, and economic forces determine the winners and losers in competition. Every winning position is unique, but all winning positions are shaped by these same natural forces. Think of this as the principle of fingerprints. Yes, all fingerprints are unique, but one fingerprint is more like an other fingerprint than it is like anything else in the world. This is because the biological forces that the create fingerprints in the womb are identical for everyone.

Our understanding of the forces involved in human competition didn't come from the study of business. In the long history of human competition, business competition has usually been below the surface of history. The science of strategy comes from the study of a far more intense and deadly form of human competition, the deadly battles of war.

Think of war as the laboratory for the science of competition. Physicists don't study the interaction of nuclear particles in their living rooms. They study them in the extreme conditions created by particle accelerators. These extreme conditions bring out the true essence of natural systems. Extreme conditions expose the underlying forces. These forces are usually invisible in everyday life because they are either disguised or taken for granted.

Though this book borrows terminology from business literature, the actual formulas on which this book is based come directly from the science of military strategy. The great works of strategy, going back 2,500 years to Sun Tzu's *The Art of War*, do not refer to specific weapons, troops, or techniques used in conflict. Instead, they deal with basic forces that shape human competition, the conditions that determine success or failure. They cover the workings of the most important competitive weapon of all, the human mind.

Because war deals with life and death, it brings the forces of competition into high relief. The science of strategy has always taken a systematic approach to understanding competition. The struggle for survival works wonderfully to concentrate the mind.

Survival is also the perfect test of ideas. Those who bring bad ideas or fuzzy thinking to the battlefield do not survive. Their books don't get passed down through the generations. When the ideas survive and the books get written, it is because they work. When the books are passed down for thousands of years, it means that, without fail, each and every generation discovered that the ideas worked for them as well.

Business is war by other means. Business competition is also war for survival. The big difference is that in business, the warriors themselves do not die. Their business enterprises, however, fall by the millions every year.

Where armies fight over physical territory, businesses battle over the marketplace. Throughout history, armies have used a variety of weapons. Businesses compete using a variety of products and business techniques as their weapons. Only the rules of strategy have remained the same.

Remember:

- ⊗ Strategy began in the life-and-death competition of war.
- ⊗ These formulas have been refined over thousands of years.
- ⊗ The Science of Strategy Institute has adapted them to business during the past few decades of working with the world's largest organizations.

The Formulas of Science

What makes these strategic formulas better than other ways of describing successful businesses?

Science is the realm of reproducible results. Science makes predictions. To make accurate predictions, you have to be precise about how a system works. This means you have to use language carefully. Mathematics is the language of science because it is more precise than spoken languages. The first works of strategy were almost as mathematical as the first works of geometry.

We use simple, direct language to describe the nine business success formulas in this book. We do not use math, but we use language in a precise way. We define the terms clearly. We could have used mathematical equations such as $P = Env(CM) / Ent((LS)^*(G(F+U)))$—a mathematical version of our 9 Key Components Formula—but these equations are too scary for most people, by which I mean they were too scary for me. Instead, we write out our formulas more like recipes, listing the ingredients

We give you all the science but none of the scary math! We make strategy as easy as baking a chocolate cake.

and how to use them.

An incomplete formula is like an incomplete bridge; it doesn't get you anywhere. Ninety percent of a working formula is worse than no formula at all. It has most of the costs, but it produces none of the benefits. For example, if you leave out the smallest part of a cake recipe, the teaspoon of baking soda, you don't get a cake. You get a pan of glop. This is a waste of all the flour, sugar, eggs, milk, salt, and whatever else you tossed in the mix.

Just because a certain ingredient is good does not mean that more of it is better. It depends on the formula you are working with. Sometimes adding more of a good ingredient will give you a better result, but more often it will create an imbalance that throws off the whole recipe. For example, sugar is good and necessary in a cake, but too much sugar can easily ruin a cake.

Remember:

- ✖ Formulas are precise, scientific descriptions.
- ✖ Formulas list all the parts required.
- ✖ Formulas detail the relationships of those parts.

Formulas to Make Success Easy

Does it require a genius to use these formulas for business success?

Any businessperson can easily understand the science of strategy. Strategy is logical. Even though this book introduces you to just the tip of the iceberg in terms of strategic thinking, you can start using these formulas right away to help you make better business decisions every day.

Most businesses are like pipelines kinked with bottlenecks. The money cannot flow through that pipeline into your wallet because it is being cut off. Think of your business as a garden hose with a kink cutting off the water. If you don't understand how garden hoses work as a system, manually fixing a kink in one place just moves the kink somewhere else. To get the water flowing, you have to understand the basic geometry of the system.

As we explain this system for competitive success, you will be able to identify where your current formula is cutting off the flow of money in your business. You can then focus your limited resources of time, effort, and money on the few key areas that really require attention at any given time.

Though we have written this book mostly in terms of building a successful business, these same ideas can be applied to advancing any competitive position. We intentionally talk about the "enterprise" and "new ventures" because any goal can be an enterprise and any campaign a new venture. If you work within a large organization, your career can be the enterprise. The steps you take to advance your career are your ventures.

Remember:

- These formulas are for everyone.
- Having a formula focuses you on what you are missing.
- The road to success starts by avoiding failure.

Formulas for a New Perspective

If these concepts make success so easy, why doesn't everyone discover them on their own?

You wouldn't discover these ideas yourself any more than you could see that the world is round without the help of Copernicus and Galileo. These ideas have been uncovered by years of scientific analysis. Learning them is like learning that the world is round, not flat. Once this is discovered, the world looks different.

Mastering the secrets of strategy is like learning to ride a bike or learning how to swim. Thinking strategically is unnatural. Our only natural instincts in competitive situations are "flight" or "fight." Once you have learned to see challenges strategically and start practicing strategic methods, thinking strategically becomes easier.

Translation: We have a lot of other books on strategy you will want to start reading when you finish this one!

However, unlike riding a bike or swimming, strategy is not just a set of physical reflexes. It is an entire school of knowledge. Mastering a strategic perspective is fairly easy, but it opens the door to an entire new world of thinking. This new world is very large indeed. You can profitably explore that world for the rest of your life.

Why is an object that lies just around the corner difficult to see? Because something blocks your vision. If you change your perspective by moving even a few inches, what was once difficult to see becomes easy to see.

Remember:

- Strategic thinking is nonintuitive and must be learned.
- Once you learn and start practicing the basics of strategy, it will become something of a habit.
- The habit of strategy opens a door to a new world.

Final Thoughts on Formulas

-⊖- The success of your business doesn't depend as much on its quality as on its fitness to compete. Your business is greater than the sum of its functional parts. A single missing part can doom the whole enterprise. The only relevant measure is how you stack up against your competition.

-⊖- All businesses have a unique business position, but all successful business positions are different. They are based on the same underlying formulas for competitive success. The dynamics of competition determine market winners and losers. You cannot simply copy another business because no two businesses can occupy the same place at the same time. You have to understand the forces shaping competitive positions.

-⊖- You find real success by making your life easier. If you don't understand the forces shaping the winners and losers in business, you cannot harness those forces. If you fight the dynamics of the marketplace, you are doomed to fail. Strategy is knowing how to leverage the opportunities all around you.

—FORMULA 1—
9 KEY
COMPONENTS

Understand Competitive Positions

You must start from where you are. This first formula explains to you exactly where you are in terms of your competitive position. The next eight formulas describe how to improve your position, but before you can build something up, you have to know what it is. This first formula breaks your position down into its nine key components for easy analysis.

This 9 Key Components Formula describes the nine parts that define every competitive position. This formula ignores the normal operational and financial view of a business. It gets at the elemental truth of what a business is and why it exists. Using it, you can understand the strengths and weaknesses of your position relative to the positions of your competitors.

Every Position Is Unique

Doesn't normal business analysis tell me my competitive position?

Normal business analysis looks at your profits and assets. Your profits are the result of a competitive position, not the position itself. Your assets go into your position, but they aren't your position. To use an analogy, knowing your car's speed and gas consumption doesn't tell you how your car works. It may tell you how well your car is running, but it doesn't tell you anything about the how gasoline is converted into speed.

At a functional level, most businesses look the same. They make or acquire products, market those products, and sell products and services. At this functional level, we evaluate businesses by their many visible features. What products do they sell? Where are they located? What are their prices? How big are they? What are their policies? What kinds of people work for them? In this functional evaluation, the key competitive issues are lost in the myriad of details.

> *Knowing how well a business is running is not the same as knowing how it works.*

All these visible differences are the result of strategic decisions. A strategic analysis of business looks at underlying causes, not the external visible effects. Again, we want to understand how the machine works, not just what it does. Strategy asks a different set of questions. Why do businesses sell the products that they do? Why are they located where they are? Why do they set certain prices and policies? Why do they hire certain kinds of people?

All these questions have a single answer. Businesses are shaped by their competitive position. The functional decisions that a business makes and the financial results of its operation arise from the basic characteristics of this position.

Most businesses fail because they don't understand their competitive position. They don't understand what a competitive position is, what it is made of, and how it works. They cannot compare their competitive position to those of their competitors. Lacking this knowledge, they are misled by appearances. Making your business appear competitive is important, but it is just part of the formula. This brings us to our first formula.

The 9 Key Components Formula

INGREDIENTS:

1) A competitive neighborhood, 2) an enterprise, 3) a business climate, 4) a marketplace, 5) leadership, 6) systems, 7) a mission, 8) unity, and 9) focus

INSTRUCTIONS:

1) Identify your competitive neighborhood and the enterprises within it. 2) Examine the external conditions of the business climate and marketplace in the competitive neighborhood. 3) For your enterprise, examine your leadership and business systems to identify their key characteristics. 4) Know the nature of your mission. 5) Evaluate how well this mission unites the organization and focuses it on its marketplace. 6) Gather outside perspectives on your competitors. 7) Compare your enterprise with its competitors' leaders, systems, and missions to determine the relative strengths and weaknesses of its competitive position. 8) Rate the reliability of information based on signs of deception or self-delusion. 9) Repeat the process after each step of progress to weight your chances of success.

9 KEYS

The rest of the chapter will explain this formula in more detail. Once you understand the nature of your competitive position, you can identify potential opportunities and evaluate the most desirable opportunities to pursue. The other formulas of strategy teach the methods for gradually improving your position over time. Advancing your position is like climbing up a ladder. The ladder must be solidly grounded on a clear understanding of your position, or it will slip out from under you.

Remember:

- ❀ Business analysis misses what makes a business work.
- ❀ Visible differences between businesses arise from their hidden differences in competitive position.
- ❀ This 9 Key Components Formula explains the differences between competing positions.

1. Identify the Competitive Neighborhood

What does my competitive neighborhood have to do with my survival?

The competitive environment is the arena in which businesses struggle to survive. Twenty-five hundred years ago, well before Darwin, strategy taught that competitive success depended upon utilizing the conditions in the environment.

Survival starts with understanding your environment and how to use its resources. Even without any competition, a business cannot survive if there is no place for it in the business environment.

Conceptually the competitive environment is infinite since human desires are infinite. In practice, however, the environment

is constrained by limitations of time and place. You can think globally, but you have to act locally. This is why we limit strategic analysis to your COMPETITIVE NEIGHBORHOOD, the part of the business environment in which you compete. Think of your neighborhood as a narrow strip of the larger competitive world.

Your competitive neighborhood is dynamic—continually changing. Traditional business planning is designed for controlled, static environments. In the competitive environment, the conflicting plans of you, your competitors, your customers, and your suppliers collide. The result is nothing that anyone could plan. Strategy was specifically designed to deal with the unpredictable nature of these dynamic, complex, uncontrolled environments.

A competitive position describes your role in the business ecosystem. Even if you have many different competitors, your role in your competitive neighborhood is unique. It is both externally and internally unique. These internal and external differences describe why your enterprise plays the role it does. They also explain why only you as an individual can play the role that you do within your enterprise.

The ENTERPRISE is what struggles for survival. Externally, your enterprise exists at a unique place and time. Just as no two objects can be in the same space at the same time, no two enterprises can offer the exact same product to the exact same customers at the exact same time. No two businesspeople can perform exactly the same tasks in the same place at the same time.

Internally, you and your enterprise have a unique set of skills and a unique personality. Real businesses are made up of real people using real equipment in real buildings. We have lots of nearly identical buildings in the world, but within those buildings each organization has a unique character, just like each person within your organization has a unique personality.

When we talk about competitive positions, we are describing a unique constellation of business relationships. This network of relationships is unbelievably complex, but fortunately we don't have to worry about all that complexity. In the end, the competitive positions of enterprises and individuals are determined by just a handful of key elements. These key elements combine together to form that galaxy of relationships in the same way that a few atomic particles combine to form all the complexity of the natural world.

An Enterprise Within Its Neighborhood

Remember:

- ✖ You focus on your position in a competitive environment.
- ✖ Your enterprise has a unique position in its neighborhood.
- ✖ That position has both external and internal aspects.

2. Examine External Conditions

What are the key external differences in my position?

The external differences in your competitive position are the customers you serve and their changing emotional attitudes. We call these two characteristics the marketplace and the business climate. These two are so intimately connected that they are just two sides of the same thing. A marketplace cannot exist without a business climate. They are very different aspects of the same thing. You will find that most concepts in strategy consist of these "complementary opposites."

The BUSINESS CLIMATE is the trends of change. Climate cannot exist without a marketplace. Climate is the emotional attitudes that affect business that change over time. The marketplace is the world of transactions that result from and affect those emotional attitudes. Climate is the general atmosphere under which business is conducted. The marketplace is the physical realm where products move from producer to consumer.

The business climate is much bigger than your position. A general business climate affects the business environment everywhere. Each business market has its own climate, just like each geographic area has its own climate. The marketplace in your business neighborhood also has its specific climate.

The MARKETPLACE is the physical world in which you interact with customers. It is the place in which the competitive battle for customers takes place. The marketplace is both where you battle the competition and what you fight to win. This battlefield exists partly on a mental plane. It consists of everything that customers and suppliers know about each other. Unlike the climate, which is largely beyond your control, the most important aspect of the marketplace is the place you choose within it.

The marketplace consists of market space. Every marketplace has size, dimension, and shape. Physically, it consists of geography. Mentally, it consists of different types of knowledge. Different groups of customers are in different "places," both physically and mentally. Theoretically, this market space is infinite, since human desire has no limit. Businesses and people can be grouped and regrouped in any different number of ways within it.

Your market position is the particular segment of that infinite market space that you choose to serve. When you choose your marketplace, you also choose your climate. The market is the realm of place. The climate is the realm of time. Like changes in the weather, changes in the attitudes are beyond your direct control. The business climate continuously swings between the extremes of desire and indifference, confidence and fear. These emotional changes have real impact on the marketplace.

The emotional nature of the climate explains many aspects of the marketplace that are poorly explained by traditional economics. For example, prices are determined primarily by climate, that is, emotion. Gas prices go up when the Middle East is threatened, even when supply and demand stay the same. The supply and demand curves are based on the physical marketplace, but it is the emotional climate that really controls what people will spend.

Though you cannot control the climate, you can foresee its changes and make decisions. On the simplest level, you decide when to open for business and when to close. You base your decision upon what you see as the best times during the day to conduct business. A bank, a restaurant, and a convenience store all make very different decisions because they operate in different climates.

Constant changes in climate means that your position is always changing as well. No position is truly stable. If you don't do anything to respond to these changes, you will become their victim instead of their master. You must always look for ways to advance your position because changes in climate are always eroding it.

Remember:

- Marketplace is the physical source of your income.
- Climate is the emotional trends of change in business.

3. Examine the Leader and Systems

What are the key internal aspects of my enterprise?

First, think about how your enterprise gets work done. Once again, there are two components—leadership and systems—and both are two sides of the same coin. An enterprise isn't an enterprise unless it has both. A person isn't in business unless he or she can make decisions and get things done. The decisions of leaders are meaningless unless they are executed though systems. The execution of systems is aimless without leadership. Successful people and organizations always make decisions in terms of what they can do. Good decisions rest on the ability to execute. Good execution depends on the ability to make good decisions.

LEADERSHIP is the internal ability to make decisions. By definition, a leader is the person within an organization who makes the key decisions. Leadership is the realm of the individual and character. Organizations and individuals vary considerably in their ability to make decisions. Successful organizations are not run by committees. They are run by strong individuals who can make good decisions. You must master the principles of strategy so that you can make the right decisions quickly.

Strategy teaches that good leadership requires five characteristics. Leaders must be be intelligent, caring, trustworthy, disciplined, and courageous. However, they must not have too much of these characteristics. This converts them into the flaws of overanalysis, oversensitivity, an overly delicate sense of honor, rigidity, and foolhardiness.

SYSTEMS are the techniques of organizations and the skills of individuals. Simply put, systems are everything that you or your business knows how to do. Systems knowledge is often embodied in machines, but machines are tools. In the end, all systems are defined by interactions or transactions among different people.

Systems are the realm of group action and interaction. Even if you are the only person in your organization, all your systems for doing business are built around working with others. No man is an island, and certainly no enterprise is an island. You need customers and suppliers to exist. Manufacturing may seem to be an internal process, but you build products to affect customers. Because systems are about interacting with people, the most important rule of your systems is that they must be in tune with your core mission.

Remember:

- Leadership is your ability to make decisions.
- Systems are the methods of interacting with others.

4. Identify the Levels of Mission

What is the core mission of an enterprise?

MISSION is the reason why enterprises and individuals do what they do. The goal is to advance your competitive position over time. Without a clear understanding of what your mission is, you cannot even define what an "advance" really means.

All businesses and people have a mission, whether they realize it or not. A mission consists of the shared goals and values that bring people together. These values join a business with its employees, customers, partners, and suppliers. A mission can be simply economic, that is, making money, but the best missions are based on higher values.

Mission gives people their motivation for doing what they do. People can have different motivations for doing the exact same thing. The nature of their motivation determines how devoted they are and how they make decisions in the future. Businesses can provide the same goods and services for radically different reasons.

Mission is the core of a competitive position. It defines the philosophical intersection between an enterprise and its environment. In illustrating the key components of a strategic position, we show mission as the nucleus around which everything else revolves.

While economic values are the most basic form of shared mission, there are three other layers of mission that are even more important. A mission can work on an economic level, a professional level, an emotional level, and a spiritual level.

The most basic level of mission is economic. Everyone shares the need for physical survival. Basic economic needs must be met in some way for an organization to survive.

On the next higher level, a professional mission develops your reputation in the marketplace. This reputation goes beyond simply offering a good product at a good price. Its earns the credibility to develop longer-lasting partnerships.

Emotional missions are built on genuine caring for others. They are founded in the value of personal relationships. This missions seek to make the world a better place for those who we love.

Spiritual missions are based on ultimate truths and eternal values. Enterprises with spiritual missions make the world a for all people everywhere forever. These high-level missions create organizations that can last thousands of years. These are the missions that people are willing to die for.

There are many "opportunities" for making money in the short term that can undermine higher level missions over the longer term.

Remember:

- Mission is your business values and goals.
- There are four different levels of mission.
- The most powerful missions focus on values.

5. Evaluate Unity and Focus

How does mission affect my enterprise?

Missions may seem idealistic, but they are very pragmatic. Idealism doesn't long survive the brutal world of warfare from which the science of strategy arose. Your mission provides your strategic position with unity and focus. Unity and focus are the source of strength in a competitive position. Experience has proven over time that if an enterprise doesn't stand apart, it soon falls apart.

A solid mission binds an enterprise together and defines its relationship with the outside world. Mission is the glue that unites an enterprise internally, binding its people together. Mission is the motivation that focuses the enterprise on a particular marketplace. Without the core of mission, the enterprise falls apart and it never finds a place within the larger market.

UNITY comes from people working together toward a common goals. Without a clear mission, even a one-person organization can

be at odds with itself. In larger enterprises, managers and employees must work together. Employees whose interests are not served by the enterprise will eventually go elsewhere. Everyone's personal goals must be satisfied by serving the mission of the enterprise.

FOCUS results from mission concentrating attention on a specific type of value for a specific type of customer. Without the focus that comes from mission, an enterprise will pursue too many different types of customers and opportunities. This weakens the organization by spreading its resources too thinly in a marketplace. A lack of focus creates external weakness in the marketplace.

Focus keeps the enterprise on track. An enterprise cannot be all things to all people. Without a clear mission, an enterprise will pull itself apart pursuing every possible opportunity. If an enterprise understands its mission, it can concentrate its resources in a smaller area. This concentration is the source of power.

A weak mission results in a weak organization. If people put their personal goals above the shared mission, their competing goals suck energy out of the organization. If people are not clear on what the big goals are, they will end up chasing their tails. Good organizations reward people for understanding and satisfying the shared mission.

Missions and values are not empty ideas. They are the framework that supports every enterprise.

Systems take on a life of their own when their goals are disconnected from the overall mission. All business functions must satisfy the core mission. This is especially true in larger organizations that have functional divisions separating product design from marketing, marketing from sales, sales from shipping, shipping from manufacturing, and manufacturing from customer support. These divisions develop their own internal goals that pull them away from the external mission. The result is a lack of focus and divisive internal politics.

Mission must also join the enterprise with the goals of the larger marketplace. Both customers and suppliers must satisfy their own needs by doing business with you. A mission isn't only needed to bring the organization together, it is needed to identify the best potential customers and partners in the marketplace.

Remember:

- ▨ Unity defines the strength of an organization.
- ▨ Focus creates strength in the marketplace.
- ▨ Both arise from your mission.

6. Get an Outside Perspective

Why can't I trust my regular contacts and instincts when evaluating my competitive position?

Your position is not determined by what you think. It is determined by what others think about you. The general view shared in the marketplace is always very different than your personal view.

It is impossible to be unbiased about your own strategic position. One of the problems is that you know too much. You naturally know a lot more about your position than you do about your competitors' positions. You know more about your position than your customers do. Your own viewpoint is the least useful in terms of understanding your true position in the competitive neighborhood.

Not only do other people not see what you see, but they see things that you can no longer see. Most retailers have shop signs. After a few years, the retailers stop seeing their signs. Instead, they remember them. They still see what they first saw when their signs were shiny and new. Every casual observer sees that sign more clearly than its owner does.

Every different position offers a different perspective. Every viewpoint is valid. Every different perspective provides a different piece of the complete picture.

Most people talk to people too much like themselves. These people share a similar perspective. You think you are getting outside opinion. You are really getting an echo.

You cannot use this formula without gathering a broad range of views about your market position and that of the competitors in your neighborhood. The more people you talk to from more groups, the better this formula works. To get this information, you must talk to customers and suppliers who deal with your competitors. To get information from your own customers and suppliers, it might be better to get some neutral third party to ask the questions.

Science is based on an unbiased analysis of the data. For an experiment to be considered valid, it has to undergo peer review. Others must be able to reproduce your results. In the science of strategy, no analysis is considered complete unless it is tested against outside opinions.

Collecting information is central to the science of strategy. It is part of every formula in this book. The next most important formula in strategy, Find Friends Formula, details the process of developing channels of communication.

Remember:

- ✹ You cannot see yourself or your competitors objectively.
- ✹ Your information sources are too close to your position.
- ✹ You need outsiders who can offer an objective perspective.

7. Compare to Competitors

How do I evaluate the quality of my competitive position?

Welcome to the world of relativity. In strategy, all factors derive their qualities from comparison. You cannot say how good or bad your enterprise is in a vacuum. The elements of your competitive position are not good or bad in themselves. They are only good or bad in comparison with the competitive positions of your competitors.

Comparing competitive positions is more revealing than comparing other isolated factors such as relative size or even products. People do not buy only because of a company's size. They do not buy simply because they prefer a particular feature in a particular product. It is always the whole package. They do business with you. You want to ask the most important question in business: why would anyone do business with you?

> *Your enterprise lives or dies based upon how it compares to its real-world competitors.*

You are only as good as your competition makes you. The only relevant comparison is with other businesses that offer realistic alternatives to your customers. Your competitive position is how the market places you in relationship with your competitors.

You never have to worry about being "perfect." Your marketplace doesn't have to be perfect. Your systems don't have to be perfect. You only have to worry about whether or not you are better than the competition.

At this point, this comparison isn't some complicated calculation. You just have to ask yourself a series of questions.

Which enterprises are in the best competitive neighborhood?
Which enterprises are the best known?
Which enterprises are leveraging changes in the climate?
Which enterprises have chosen the best market segments?
Which enterprises make the best decisions most rapidly?
Which enterprises have the most effective and efficient systems?
Which enterprises have the clearest and highest-level missions?
Which enterprises have the most united teams of people?
Which enterprises have the sharpest focus on the market?

You just rate yourself and your competitors from the best to the worst in each of these nine categories. Answer these questions as honestly as you can. If you don't know the answer to most of these questions, you cannot know your competitive position. The difference between successful businesspeople and unsuccessful people is that successful people know the answers to these questions. Unsuccessful people never even think to ask them.

You don't have to be the best in all nine areas. Your first priority is just to know honestly where you stand. The goal is to be competitive in every area and have an advantage in more areas than anyone else.

For now, the point is knowing where you are behind. Your enterprise will not succeed just because you plan to work harder than your competitors. You can easily put a lot of hard work into developing the wrong area. The secret of competitive positioning is balance. You cannot be so weak in any area that you are not competitive. You don't want to waste time perfecting one element at the risk of neglecting the others. The secret to success is putting the right effort into the right place at the right time.

Remember:
- ⊗ The quality of your position is relative to that of competitors.
- ⊗ Each of the nine factors must be compared.
- ⊗ This analysis must be ongoing.

8. Examine for Deception and Delusion

How much faith can I put in my competitive analysis?

The question is, how much of that position is based upon reality and how much upon appearances? People never know the truth. We have only our perceptions. Perception is reality. Customers make their buying decisions based solely upon their perceptions.

This raises two questions. Do your competitors get high marks from the marketplace because they are better at controlling appearances? Do you get a lower market share because your are poor at controlling customer perceptions? Understanding the difference is important. It is faster, easier, and less costly to change people's perceptions than it is to change the reality. If people's positive view of your competitors is based on appearances, it will fade with time.

You always have to be concerned with the impression you make on people. If your enterprise seems too new, you want to appear more experienced. If it appear sloppy, you want it to look organized. If your enterprise appears like it is struggling, you can make it appear as though you are successful. If your enterprise appears amateurish, you want it to appear more professional. Appearances are important and relatively easy to fix.

You can use appearances to create a satisfying experience. If you are selling your newness, you must appear new. If you are selling your experience, you must look experienced. If what you are is at odds with how you appear, creating misleading impressions works against you.

If your competitors rate higher because they have a good but false front, perception will take care of itself over time, but that may not help you. Experience trumps appearance. As people gain experience, appearances matter less and less. However, if you are not careful about offering a good appearance, you will not survive long enough for people to discover the truth about your competitors.

Bad news: Everybody lies! Good news: In the long run, everybody finds out the lies! Bad news: In the long run, we're all dead!

There is one last use for illusion. As you are evaluating your competitors, your competitors are also evaluating you. If possible, you want to mislead your competition about the true nature of your business. You want to appear less threatening than you are. You want to appear less important than you are. You want your appearance to mislead or at least confuse them about what you are really trying to accomplish.

It is best if you can create three different sets of impressions. You want your potential customers see you one way initially to bring them in. While that initial impression attracts customers, you want your competitors to see it as irrelevant in the long term. Over time, you want your customers to develop a deeper understanding of what your enterprise can do for them. This deeper threat should be hidden from your competitors.

The power of controlling perceptions is that potential competitors cannot copy it because they don't really see it clearly.

Remember:

- ⊗   Everyone offers only opinions, not the objective truth.
- ⊗   The reality of your competitive position is subjective.
- ⊗   Changing opinions is the same as changing positions.

9. Repeat the Analysis

How can you tell me about recursive algorithms without making it sound like a bunch of big words?

You must test and retest your competitive position. The market is always changing. Even if you have had a relatively strong position in the past and you haven't changed it, it is degrading because your competitors are working to improve their positions.

This is why you must constantly work to advance your position. The eight formulas that follow put you on the path to finding, picking, and exploiting the best opportunities for advancing your position. After each of these steps, you want to spend at least a few moments rethinking your position. You have to always keep in mind what your new position is.

Before undertaking any new venture, you must know that you can make a profit. You can only make a profit if your competitive position in that venture gives you an advantage. Before you get into a venture, you look at how you are positioning yourself. This analysis may show that your idea has too many flaws. You want to avoid any venture that weakens your competitive position.

Weak positions hurt your chances of survival. New ventures based on weak positions are a waste of resources. In a poor business climate, you cannot survive business droughts. In a poor marketplace, you have too few potential customers. If your leadership is weak, you respond too slowly to changes. If your business systems are weak, you have high costs and undependable quality. The goal of any new venture is to make you stronger. Weak attempts to advance your position weaken your position.

You can predict your success or failure before you undertake any new venture. If your venture isn't competitive in every key element and superior in at least some from a customer's perspective, that venture will certainly fail. The more key areas in which you have an advantage, the more likely success will be.

Your first responsibility is to make the safe decisions. You cannot make a safe decision without comparing your elemental position with your competitors' positions. You should not even try to compete with competitors whose business formulas you do not understand.

In the end, you must make decisions. It takes a great deal of knowledge to be successful in business. There are limits to what you can know. This formula identifies the nine categories of information that are the key to making good business decisions. There are an infinite number of business details that you can safely ignore. Just get the feel for the business climate, your competitive neighborhood, its enterprises, their philosophies, their market segments, their leadership, and their systems and compare your venture with that of your competition.

Remember:

- Your competitive position is always changing.
- Analysis predicts which ventures will be profitable.
- Success comes from a clear competitive advantage.

Final Thoughts on Key Components

-⊙-   Strong competitive positions come from a balance of strong components. The elements that make up your position determine its underlying strength. Competitive skill is terrific, but everyone makes mistakes. A solid competitive position will survive despite your mistakes.

-⊙-   By using this formula, you make certain that your enterprise doesn't have any fatal flaws. If your business is based on a weak philosophy, an uncertain climate, a difficult market, indecisive leadership, or unworkable systems, you cannot work hard enough or smart enough to make the venture succeed. If your business has a strong philosophy, a predictable climate, a good market, skilled leadership, and solid systems, you can survive a lot of mistakes.

-⊙-   The most easily overlooked part of this formula is your core mission. Your mission is the basis of everything else. The goals of your mission focus you on the best opportunities. They allow you to weather the storms in the business climate. Your values unite everyone who is touched by your enterprise. Values are the basis of businesses that work over time.

-⊙-   You must know where your competitors stand to know where you stand. Your position takes its relative strengths and weaknesses from its relationship with your competitors. Customers choose from real alternatives. Your competitors are constantly educating them about what those alternatives are. As long as your competitors are active, your competitive position is changing. You must work to advance it as competitors work to undermine it.

More About The 9 Key Components

This chapter has been expanded into the first volume of a nine-volume work on strategy called Sun Tzu's Playbook. *The articles in this volume are listed below.*

1.0.0 Competitive Positioning: Sun Tzu's eight keys to understanding competitive strategy in terms of developing relatively superior positions.

1.1.0 Position Paths: Sun Tzu's six keys to understanding the continuity of strategic positions over time.

1.1.1 Position Dynamics: Sun Tzu's seven keys to understanding how all current positions are always getting better or worse.

1.1.2 Defending Positions: Sun Tzu's six keys to understanding the basic ways that we defend our current positions until new positions are established.

1.1.3 Resisting Advances: Sun Tzu's eight keys to the most effective ways for advancing competitive positions.

1.2 Subobjective Positions: Sun Tzu's eight keys to understanding the subjective and objective aspects of a position.

1.2.1 Competitive Landscapes: Sun Tzu's seven keys to understanding the arenas in which rivals jockey for position.

1.2.2 Exploiting Exploration: Sun Tzu's seven keys to knowing how competitive landscapes are searched and positions utilized.

1.2.3 Position Complexity: Sun Tzu's seven keys to understanding how strategic positions arise from interactions in complex environments.

1.3 Elemental Analysis: Sun Tzu's eight keys to understanding the relevant components of all competitive positions.

1.3.1 Competitive Comparison: Sun Tzu's six keys to understanding competition as the comparison of positions.

1.3.2 Element Scalability: Sun Tzu's six keys to understanding how positions are analyzed by both component positions and elements.

1.4 The External Environment: Sun Tzu's seven keys to understanding the key external conditions shaping strategic positions.

1.4.1 Climate Shift: Sun Tzu's nine key keys to understanding forces of environmental change shaping temporary conditions.

1.4.2 Ground Features: Sun Tzu's ten keys to understanding the persistent resources that we can control.

1.5 Competing Agents: Sun Tzu's seven keys to understanding characteristics of competitors.

1.5.1 Command Leadership: Twelve keys to understanding individual decision-making (leaders).

1.5.2. Group Methods: Sun Tzu's ten keys to understanding systems for executing decisions (skills).

1.6 Mission Values: Sun Tzu's eight keys to the goals and values needed for motivation.

1.6.1 Shared Mission: Sun Tzu's ten keys to finding goals that others can share.

1.6.2 Types of Motivations: Sun Tzu's six keys to understanding hierarchies of motivation that define missions.

1.6.3 Shifting Priorities: Sun Tzu seven keys to how missions change according to temporary conditions.

1.7 Competitive Power: Sun Tzu's ten keys to understanding the sources of superiority in challenges.

1.7.1 Team Unity: Sun Tzu's ten keys to increasing our strength by the way we join with others.

1.7.2 Goal Focus: Five keys to understanding strength as arising from concentrating efforts.

1.8 Progress Cycle: Sun Tzu's ten keys to understanding the adaptive loop by which positions are advanced.

1.8.1 Creation and Destruction: Sun Tzu's five keys to the creation and destruction of competitive positions.

1.8.2 The Adaptive Loop: Sun Tzu's eight keys to the continual reiteration of position analysis.

1.8.3 Cycle Time: Sun Tzu's four keys to understanding the importance of speed in feedback and reaction.

1.8.4 Probabilistic Process: Sun Tzu's six keys to understanding the role of chance in strategic processes and systems.

1.9 Competition and Production: Sun Tzu's seven keys to understanding the two opposing skill sets of competition and production.

1.9.1 Production Comparisons: Sun Tzu's six keys to understanding how production naturally creates competition.

1.9.2 Span of Control: Sun Tzu's eight keys to understanding the boundaries of competition and production.

—FORMULA 2—

FIND FRIENDS

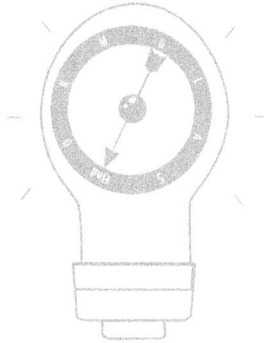

Success Starts With Information

After you understand your competitive position, you must take the first step to improve it. You start making friends. You don't make friends to become popular, but to win information and become better known. Successful businesspeople know that information is power. This knowledge doesn't come from books or media. Successful people know how to find friends.

Before you can advance your position, you must first develop a network of friends. Most people don't have enough relationships. Many people don't have the right relationships. Some people do not know how to use relationships. The Find Friends Formula teaches you the pattern of successful relationships. It shows you how to harnesses the most powerful competitive weapon of all: the human mind.

Friendship Is a Competitive Weapon

Are people who are successful at competition better liked than their competitors or more hated?

Friendship, in the sense we are using it, isn't about being liked or hated. It is about knowing people and being known. It is especially about being practical in your need for information. You need information every day. Even the smallest business enterprise can affect the lives of thousands of people. Even the simplest business involves making the same types of decisions over and over again. All businesses continually consume time, energy, and money. You must know what changes in the marketplace can affect them.

Your business is always at risk. Failure is always a possibility. You can always make mistakes that threaten your business, but your business is in danger even if you operate it perfectly. Changes in the marketplace or business climate can put you out of business. A new competitor can open next door tomorrow. New technology can revolutionize an industry overnight.

Your existing competitive position is constantly eroding. You have to constantly work to improve your competitive position, and improving, expanding, and building up your business is costly. Most of your new ideas will fail to pay for themselves. Only a precious few will be successful.

You can run a business for years. Then a single opportunity can come along and change everything. You must choose whether to embrace that opportunity or to reject it. If the opportunity proves to be false, embracing it will cost you everything that you built up over the years. If the opportunity proves to be your big chance at success, rejecting it may lead inevitably to failure.

You have to make the right decisions every day. Despite this, many businesspeople invest their time, money, and effort in advertising, inventory, and systems, but they don't invest in building their channels of information. The result can be devastating.

Without the right information, you cannot compete. You cannot develop a competitive position that attracts customers. You cannot run a business profitably. It doesn't matter how hard you work, without the right information, you will always be doing the wrong things at the wrong times.

The Find Friends Formula

INGREDIENTS:

1) A focus on the future, 2) a range of contacts, 3) old pros, 4) young fools, 5) customer connections, 6) competitor contacts, 7) missionaries, 8) a sense of value, and 9) (optional) a specific opportunity

INSTRUCTIONS:

1) Develop a preference for getting information directly from people. 2) Look for a range of contacts. 3) Get to know some old business pros. 4) Get in regular contact with young people. 5) Make a connection with your customers. 6) Contact your competitors' contacts. 7) Develop your missionaries. 8) Invest time in maintaining relationships. 9) When targeting a specific opportunity, extend your information network to gather specific information.

Remember:
- Communication is primarily used to gather information.
- Information is primarily used to control costs and risk.
- The key form of communication is listening to people.

1. Develop a Preference for People

Can't I get the information I need from reports?

All your success is in the future. All competitive decisions are made in the face of an uncertain future. A preference for people develops naturally from a FOCUS ON THE FUTURE. This is the first ingredient in the Find Friends Formula. You must know the latest ideas in your industry. You must keep in touch with where your competitors are going. You must foresee the future to put your resources in the right places at the right times.

These decisions require advance information. You need to know what people are thinking and planning. You must learn about market experiments and product trials before the results are generally available. You want to know when decision-makers are revising past decisions. You need to foresee when events are approaching the tipping point, taking the market in new directions.

You won't get this advance information from inside your enterprise. It isn't on your internal computer systems. Your employees and coworkers have no clues.

You also can't get this advance information from the outside media. It won't be in the newspapers or trade magazines. You can't find it searching the Internet.

The easy decisions are about the past. This is because it is so easy to get information out about the past. All your regular sources of information are plugged into the past. If you are willing to listen at all, you can learn from past mistakes. Decisions to fix recurring problems, the basis of the quality movement, require

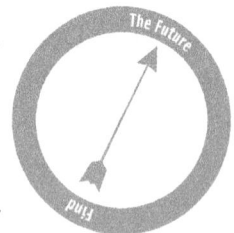

a system and discipline, but not a great network of personal contacts.

The tough decisions are all about the future. The past doesn't tell you what is changing. You cannot get advance information from past experience. You cannot reason out what is happening in the marketplace. Business theory doesn't give you a clue. You must gather information about what people are thinking and planning. You can get information from only one place—by talking to people every day.

People make their plans based on the business climate. What is the climate? It is how people feel about the future. Facts are great, but people make decisions about the future based upon feeling. Strategy leverages human psychology, and the only way you can find out what is going on in people's heads is to talk to them regularly.

Emotions are powerful. We use our emotions to gauge the future. No computer can to duplicate this power.

People who are repeatedly successful in business have one thing in common: they have the habit of developing valuable relationships. They have discovered the formula for developing the personal contacts who bring them advance information. Good contacts bring you what you need to know before you even know that you need it.

Our second strategic formula develops a people network that no computer network can equal. It not only gathers data but uses the unequalled processing power of the human brain to process it. Nothing is more valuable than getting others to care about what you need to know. You can rely upon your own brain alone. Or you can put the brains of others to work for you.

Remember:

- ✸ You need information that isn't available to everyone.
- ✸ Most information in trade magazines is irrelevant to you.
- ✸ You need to know about changes before they happen.

2. Look for a Range of Contacts

Why do you have to turn making friends into work?

Developing a broad RANGE OF CONTACTS is work. It doesn't happen naturally. You have to do it consciously. When it comes to building a contact network, all people are not created equal. Different people know different things. One well-connected person—in a network sense, not a mob sense—is worth a dozen regular contacts. Someone who knows what's going on and has unique insights is worth a dozen—no, make that a thousand—people who think like everyone else.

There are plenty of people with unique insights who don't know what is going on. We call them nuts.

Your time is limited. You have to go for quality and not quantity. Surprisingly, high-quality contacts are easy to find. People who maintain lots of contacts are, by definition, easy to make contact with. And people who think differently are not all that popular and are hungry for relationships. Either way, you can find the people you need.

Most people build their contact networks haphazardly. If they categorize people at all, it is by the interests that they share. In other words, most people tend to know people who have a similar perspective. This is great, but you don't develop a robust communication network by knowing people like yourself.

If everyone you know knows what you know, it does not matter how many people you know. If you don't know, they don't have the information either. This isn't the way successful people operate. If you copy successful people, you cultivate a variety of relationships. Then, when you want a particular type of information, you know the best person to go to to get it.

You need to gather information more effectively than the average person. You need access to information that others do not have. You want to develop a well-rounded perspective on your situation. To get a complete picture of your competitive position, you need to consciously develop ongoing relationships with five different types of people.

Five specific types of relationships are demanded by this formula. There are also specific rules for cultivating these relationships.

Remember:
- People are only equal under the law.
- Some types of diversity are superior to others.
- You need five key types of people.

3. Know the Old Pros

If the key information is about the future, how can people who know mostly about the past help me?

OLD PROS are businesspeople with a track record of experience. There is no more important teacher in business than experience—other than this book, of course. Most people learn strategy through painful trial and error because they don't have this book. The longer people survive in the world of business, the more they learn.

People who have been in business or, even better, in a specific industry, for a long time learn information that you can't get anywhere else. They may not relate to the latest developments, but they develop a depth of understanding that is invaluable. Everything that is happening now in your industry has happened before. It was in a little different form, but everything that is old is new again.

People who have been around a long time also have had a long time to get to know a lot of other people. This makes gossip more interesting for them. They know the people involved.

These people are especially good sources of connection within your industry. Rumors pass information about the industry's interesting developments long before it hits the trades.

It is easy to find old pros because they are, well, older. They stand out in a crowd. Trade associations and trade shows are a great place to meet old pros and develop these relationships.

If you regularly seek out older businesspeople, you can stumble onto a highly successful mentor.

Suppliers are another great source for old pros. Salespeople who have been able to survive are exceptionally good contacts. They also have an incentive to develop a relationship with you.

When you seek out older people, tell them that you value their experience. You will make a positive impression. Modern society has a foolish way of kicking older people to the side of the road. Most older people would love the opportunity to pass on what they know.

Remember:
- ✖ You cannot buy experience, but you can befriend it.
- ✖ Too many people overlook that value of experience.
- ✖ This creates an opportunity for you.

4. Contact Some Young Fools

Doesn't the media already flood me with news about what is new?

YOUNG FOOLS are those who see the changes in climate with fresh eyes. The media write about what interests the media. You sit in a small corner of a very large business environment. The changes of climate ripple back and forth, from one end to the other. They can reach you from any direction. As you focus on your little corner, you don't see them coming. If those changes don't fit into the media's view of what is important, they don't see them either.

Hot trends sweep through the culture. They start outside your little world. These trends can help or hinder you. You don't know from which direction they will come. The iPod did not start in the recording industry but it completely reshaped it. Starbucks did not arise from the coffee industry. It wasn't a traditional coffee or donut shop, but it change them all.

You must recognize those trends. You must prepare for them. They are where your opportunity lies.

Most businesspeople are not plugged into the hot trends. This is why so many see the business world as boring. Most businesspeople are focused on the work at hand. There is always plenty of that. They are more worried about the problems that happened yesterday than the opportunities that will open tomorrow.

To be open to what is happening in the world, you have to have an empty mind. Businesspeople have a lot on their minds. Who has the emptiest minds in the world?

While you are thinking about that question also consider that keeping track of the world of change is also time consuming. Most changes are meaningless. Businesspeople are, well, busy. Who has the time to keep in touch with these trends? Who has an empty head, uh, open mind, with a lot of time to waste—I mean, invest?

Teenagers, of course.

Teenagers waste—I mean, invest—an extraordinary amount of time talking. A large percentage of their communication is about what is new. Teenagers are probably the most underutilized market research force in the world. There is a reason.

Young people have the biggest stake in the future and the most interest in learning what's new.

All contact with teens poses a challenge. If you are the parent of a teen, I'm not telling you anything you don't know. A host of cultural and psychological barriers block communication between teens and adults. It takes a little strategy to break through these barriers.

You might be fortunate. Parents can establish good communication with their teens. If you are one of those fortunate few, you get regular intelligence about what is new, whether you want it or not. If there is a secret here, it is not to tune them out. Face it. Teens aren't going to tell you what you want to know as a parent. The stuff that they are willing to talk about isn't nearly so boring if you listen like a business person instead of a parent.

Try to get them interested in the business aspects of culture. It's worth a try. It will be more difficult to get them interested in your own business, but it is worth a shot as well. I could never do it with my daughter, but it would be great if your teens could see the connection between what you do and the money they have to spend.

Of course, not everyone has teenage children. Even if you do, they do grow up—though that seems to be taking longer and longer. Then you need a different point of contact. You can reach out to your employees or business associates who have teenagers. You can establish teen advisory groups. You can tell them something that they haven't heard before—that you are interested in what they think. It doesn't hurt to feed them and bribe them with gifts.

Even easier, you can volunteer to work with teens. For a long time, I worked in Junior Achievement. It brought me into high school and junior high school classrooms. Under the guise of teaching them about business, I regularly talked to classrooms full of teens.

When talking to teens, I always ask them about what they see as new and interesting. Steer the discussion to how stupid adults are and how smart teenagers are. Talk about what teens understand that adults just don't get.

Any role that puts you in regular communication with teenagers is going to teach you more than thousands of pages of market research.

Remember:

- The world is small and it's changing quickly.
- There is always something new and hot somewhere.
- Young fools will know about what is new before you do.

5. Connect With Customers

Doesn't everyone say I should listen to my customers to the point that I am tired of hearing it?

CUSTOMER CONNECTIONS are customers you know as people. It is a tired truism that you should listen to your customers. But all of us are customers. As a customer, how many businesses do you deal with regularly? Dozens? Hundreds? How many of those businesses do you think listen to your complaints and suggestions? Or even really want to hear them? So much for listening to customers.

If a customer says, "I want to make a really, really big purchase, if you do such and so," then businesspeople listen. In the normal course of business, most information from customers just gets filtered out by the system.

Who doesn't like getting special attention? Who doesn't like to be treated like a person instead of a customer?

It's great if your business has a personal relationship with its customers. Customers with a sense of exclusive membership are devoted. However, beyond those types of customer relationships, you want to develop close contact with at least a handful of your customers—friendships close enough that they personally care about you and your success in business.

As you get to know your customers on a personal level, you get more insight into their needs and concerns. Having a range of customers as friends helps you understand that all customers are not the same. You learn what they have in common and how they are different. Ask them all what they have on their minds.

Customers who are also friends will think about your business a different way. They will be honest with you. They may even look for favors, but from the favors they ask, you will learn what customers are really looking for but not getting from your business.

You want to keep these friendships private. You do not want your business to treat your friends any differently than other customers.

Remember:

- Casual customers seldom tell you what you need to know.
- People tend to filter out what they hear every day.
- It takes time to see through customers' eyes.

6. Contact Competitors' Contacts

Why does learning about my competitors make me uncomfortable?

COMPETITOR CONTACTS are people in touch with your competition. Nothing is as important as knowing your competition. However, most people are uncomfortable learning about their competitors. Competition is an implicit form of criticism. Competitors provide what you do but differently. This implies that you are doing it wrong. Most people do not look for criticism.

The result is that most businesspeople study their competitors from a safe distance.

Get to know your competitors on a personal level. You'll see them differently. You'll see that they aren't your enemies. You have more in common with them than anyone. However, you don't necessarily get the best information from them. Competitors aren't known for being honest with one another, nor should they be.

The best information about your competitors comes from those who do business with them.

Employees and former employees of competitors are good sources. Successful people regularly hire away their competitors' best employees. Of course that won't endear you to your competitors, but it is a terrific source of inside information.

Your competitors' customers and suppliers are also important sources of information.

Competitors' customers will naturally be suspicious of your overtures. They will think that you want to win their business, not their friendship. You can let them think this. It is often easier to get competitive information if people misunderstand your motives.

Competitors' suppliers are by far the easiest source of information. They have their own motivation for building a relationship. You can open the communication channel based upon the fact that they are looking to win your business. After that, it is largely a matter of keeping it open.

If you are serious about these relationships, you will develop them over time. They can evolve from their original basis as potential customers or potential suppliers to personal friendships. This is where these contacts pay off.

Remember:

- Your competitors have the same needs that you do.
- Direct relationships with competitors are problematic.
- You must communicate with those who work with them.

7. Recruit Some Missionaries

Doesn't advertising my company and its products play any role in my communication formula?

MISSIONARIES are those who carry your message to the marketplace. Success is 80 percent listening and 20 percent promotion. The four groups discussed thus far are sources. This last group shares SENSE OF VALUE with the world.

In business school, "communication strategy" comes down to advertising. Advertising is overrated and overpriced. It is sometimes a necessary evil, but if you need to advertise, you will know it.

The best promotion is flesh and blood and brains. Success is not only who you know but who knows you. People and word of mouth are the most powerful form of advertising. Huge successes are created every day without the benefit of any advertising at all.

There are key characters in word-of-mouth communication. Malcolm Gladwell, in his book *The Tipping Point*, explains that some people are extraordinarily well connected to a large number of others. As he says, "Sprinkled in every walk of life...are a handful of people with an extraordinary knack of making friends and acquaintances." He calls these people "connectors."

You don't need to be a connector. You just need to connect with the connectors. You don't need a big Rolodex. You need to know people with big Rolodexes.

You never use connector relationships to advertise your products. Of the three P's of marketing—product, price, and promotion—only product can be communicated through people connections. A much better focus, however, is your mission.

Connectors are great missionaries. When they talk about you, you want them to focus on your core philosophy, values, and goals. Wrap your mission up in juicy bits of information. The details aren't important. Your goal is to make your mission interesting.

The higher the level of your mission, the better this works. The economics of making money are—shall I say it?—a little boring. Your professional reputation isn't much more interesting. Where you want to affect people is on the emotional and even spiritual level. Now, for a business person, that is interesting. The more emotional and the more spiritual, the better. This is the stuff that makes good stories. Connectors are always looking for good stories to tell.

In my own case, I like connectors to know about my battle with cancer. It was that battle that made me refocus my life on teaching strategy to regular people. Before, I just flew around the world teaching the corporate fat cats. Of course, I still do, but that isn't why I write books like this.

To develop relationships with connectors, make it personal. Tell your life story. Make it emotional; talk about the joy and pain. Make it spiritual. Don't get caught up in the specifics of this religion or that, but talk about the sense of human spirit and destiny that we all share.

Remember:

- Advertising is sometimes necessary but always costly.
- The communication formula is personal, not impersonal.
- Your personal message should be focused on mission.

8. Invest the Time

How does the communication formula pay if I have to spend all this time keeping in contact with all these people?

Success comes from getting the right information and knowing how to use it. Nothing is as valuable to your eventual success as information. Gathering information saves time, resources, and effort. The old saying is that tt takes money to make money. The truth is that it takes information to make money. Money is information. The profit your business makes measures precisely how much more you know than your competitors. The better your information, the better your decisions. The better your decisions, the bigger your profit.

You must reward people for providing you the right information. You want to provide them an incentive to think about you. When they hear information that might be valuable, you want them to pass it on. No reward is too generous when it comes to getting the right information at the right time.

Most communication doesn't produce valuable information directly. Your contact network gathers pieces of the puzzle. You must be smart enough to put together the pieces into a useful picture. If you are not sensitive to subtleties, you will not distill knowledge from communication. You must pay attention to small details. Each person speaks in his or her own language.

There is no such thing as contradictory information. There are only missing pieces to the puzzle. This is where contacts from a variety of different areas are helpful. Creating a complete picture takes work. You need to factor in people's motivations. Then you must filter out their prejudices. You must make sure that your own prejudices don't get in the way as you are doing this. You must be open and unbiased to evaluate what you hear.

Information can make you successful and it can cost you your success. Communication can only pay if you do not make costly mistakes by letting out the wrong information at the wrong time.

Nothing is as sensitive as confidential communication. You must respect people's need for privacy. They must respect your need for confidentiality. You must use your contacts to gather information for your business, but they must not share what you are interested in with others. Contacts who discuss your strategy with others, especially competitors, must be cut out of your network.

Remember, the formula is 80 percent listening and only 20 percent talking. Listening is always profitable and never costly. Talking can be costly if the wrong information gets to the wrong person at the wrong time. If you limit your talking to issues of mission and philosophy, it minimizes the danger, but the less you say, the better.

Remember:

❖   Nothing is as valuable as the right information.

❖   Communication must be transformed into information.

❖   You must keep information confidential.

Even if you're not a people person, making friends in a new area is easy because people like to help.

8. Extend Your Network Into Opportunities

When do I absolutely need to use this formula to expand my contact channels?

We are back again at the fascinating topic of recursive algorithms. You must start with contacts to learn about new opportunities. When you identify a SPECIFIC OPPORTUNITY that you want to explore, expand your communication channels into that area to get more information. Contact channels aren't as central to advancing your position as your position itself. I guess that's obvious. But though this is the first step, it is also a continuous process.

It doesn't matter what type of expansion you plan. You may want to target a new group of customers. You may want to take the lead in a new product category. You may want to move into a new geographical territory. Before you begin any of these campaigns, you must first develop your contacts.

Before you move into a new area, you must know who your competitors will be. You develop your contacts to find out about the competition. You must know how competitors are defending their position. You must understand how they are organized. You must discover where their key customers and suppliers are.

You want to know where your competitors get their information so you can win their information sources over. You want to talk to their employees, customers, and suppliers. In strategy, we call this getting inside their communication channels.

Moving into new areas is always costly, but good information can dramatically reduce the costs. This means that you must be willing to pay the price—in time, effort, and even dollars—for access to information. You must develop contacts who know your competitors. You especially want to find contacts who can act as your missionaries within a market.

You must do this carefully and avoid making mistakes. You can hire from within the industry and from your competitors to win competitive knowledge. You must do this selectively.

The more people you know and the more people who know you, the more opportunities you will have.

You create an image by identifying the connectors. You can control the perceptions of the trade media by introducing yourself in the right way at the right time. You get people on your side by enticing them with your vision and mission. You must do this carefully as well. You want potential customers, not the competition, to start paying attention to you.

Use the five types of contacts as a major part of your personal network, especially when you explore new areas. Use them all. The most important are those who can give you insight into your competitors. It is impossible to invest too much time in understanding in advance what your competitors are doing.

Remember:

- ✖ Your success depends on expanding your business.
- ✖ Communication channels are expanded in new areas first.
- ✖ The flow of information precedes the flow of money.

Final Thoughts on Finding Friends

⊖ Advancing your position always starts by improving your communication channels. If you study the most successful people in business, you will notice that they are always better at listening than their competitors. They listen to a wide variety of voices and are always minimizing the mistakes they make by taking the time and effort to gather information.

⊖ You must be informed. Your capabilities as a business leader depend on your channels of information. Good leaders are those who get their information from the best sources. You get the best information from the smartest people.

⊖ Who you know may or may not offer you a big opportunity, but the information that you get from them will lead you to the best opportunities. You can only survive the challenges of the marketplace if you have good market intelligence. Your enterprise's current position and future advances depend on good information sources.

More About The Find Friends Formula

This chapter has been expanded into the second volume of a nine-volume work on strategy called Sun Tzu's Playbook. *The articles in this volume are listed below.*

2.0.0 Developing Perspective: Sun Tzu seven keys to adding depth to competitive analysis.

2.1 Information Value: Sun Tzu's six keys to understanding knowledge and communication as the basis of strategy.

2.1.1 Information Limits: Sun Tzu's eight keys to making good decisions with limited information.

2.1.2 Leveraging Uncertainty: Sun Tzu's five keys to leveraging the elemental nature of uncertainty.

2.1.3 Strategic Deception: Sun Tzu nine keys to using misinformation and disinformation in competition.

2.1.4 Surprise: Sun Tzu's five keys to the creation of surprise depends on the nature of information.

2.2 Information Gathering: Sun Tzu five keys to gathering competitive information.

2.2.1 Personal Relationships: Sun Tzu's five keys to seeing why information depends on personal relationships.

2.2.2 Mental Models: Sun Tzu's five keys to knowing how mental models simplify decision-making.

2.2.3 Standard Terminology: Sun Tzu five keys to understanding how mental models must be shared to enable communication.

2.3 Personal Interactions: Sun Tzu's six keys to making progress through personal interactions.

2.3.1 Action and Reaction: Sun Tzu's eight keys to knowing how we advance based on how others reaction to our actions.

2.3.2 Reaction Unpredictability: Sun Tzu's seven keys to explaining why we can never exactly predict the reactions of others.

2.3.3 Likely Reactions: Seven keys to understanding the range of potential reactions in gathering information.

2.3.4 Using Questions: Sun Tzus five keys to using questions in gathering information and predicting reactions.

2.3.5 Infinite Loops: Four principles predicting reactions on the basis of the "you-know-that-I-know-that-you-know" problem.

2.3.6 Promises and Threats: Sun Tzu's six keys to the use of promises and threats as strategic moves.

2.4 Contact Networks: Five keys to understanding the range of contacts needed to create perspective.

2.4.1 Ground Perspective: Sun Tzu's three keys to getting information on a new competitive arena.

2.4.2 Climate Perspective: Sun Tzu's four keys to getting perspective on temporary external conditions.

2.4.3 Command Perspective: Sun Tzu's six keys to understanding developing sources for understanding decision-makers.

2.4.4 Methods Perspective: Sun Tzu's five keys to developing contacts who understand best practices.

2.4.5 Mission Perspective: Sun Tzu's seven keys to knowing how we develop and use a perspective on motivation.

2.5 The Big Picture: Sun Tzu's nine keys to building big picture strategic awareness.

2.6 Knowledge Leverage: Sun Tzu's five keys to getting competitive value out of knowledge.

2.7 Information Secrecy: Sun Tzu's nine keys to understanding the role of secrecy in relationships.

—FORMULA 3—
OBSERVE
OPPORTUNITIES

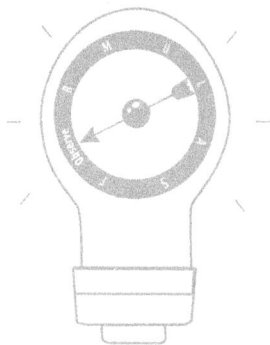

Competitors Create Your Openings

After collecting information, you use the information to identify opportunities. This raises the question: what is an opportunity? The simplest definition is an opening in the market into which you can expand and build up your position. You can only move into that space if it is open. This is why we use the term *opening* to describe strategic opportunities.

Success requires improving your position, moving from one opportunity to a better one. To move forward, you must find opportunities. These openings are stepping-stones to success. The Observe Opportunities Formula reveals the right times, proper conditions, and best places to find opportunities.

The Opportunity Formula

If I want to be successful, don't I need to learn how to create my own opportunities?

To make progress, you need an opening. Openings are empty spaces in the market. They are areas that are being overlooked by competitors. These spaces are not empty because of what you do or do not do. They are empty because of what everyone else is doing or not doing.

There are three important points that you should know about opportunities before proceeding.

1. *You* cannot create opportunity.
2. You cannot *create* opportunity.
3. You cannot create *opportunity*.

First, *you* cannot create opportunity. The competitive environment creates opportunities. Changes in the business climate create opportunities. Openings are conditions in the business environment. You do not control conditions in the business environment. The environment is very large. The largest business is microscopic by comparison. Thinking that you can create an opportunity in the business environment is like a drop of water thinking that it can change the tides of the ocean.

The dynamic forces of the competitive environment create openings.

Second, you cannot *create* opportunity. The formula teaches you to *see* opportunities, not to *create* them. Recognizing opportunities is difficult enough because it looks like nothing. Creating opportunities is impossible. See the previous point for reference.

Finally, you cannot create *opportunity*. To become successful, you have to create different conditions. In this book, we have formulas for creating communication networks, momentum, sales, and lots of other good stuff. When you think about opportunity, you cannot think about what you need to do to create it. Instead, you have to think about how you recognize it.

Openings are like a black hole. There isn't anything to see. There are no competitors, no products, and no money being made. You cannot see nothing. Like a black hole, we must recognize an opening by what it happening around it.

The Observe Opportunities Formula

INGREDIENTS:

1) Excess resources, 2) competitors in the market, 3) known strengths of competitors, 4) your mission, 5) your resource fit, and 6) first-mover advantage

INSTRUCTIONS:

1) Defend your current position. 2) Avoid direct competition. 3) Use the size of big competitors against them. 4) Use your competitors' strengths against them. 5) Move into openings quietly. 6) Focus where competitors cannot. 7) Judge opportunities using your mission, your resource fit, and your time advantage. 8) Be patient and wait until the opportunity is too obvious to pass up.

Remember:
- You cannot create opportunities.
- Opportunities must be created for you by others.
- Your job is to recognize opportunities using this formula.

1. Defend Your Current Position

Don't I need to pursue opportunities whenever they come my way?

Your first responsibility is to defend your existing position. Business is a game you can only play while you have money. When you run out, the game is over. Income is the lifeblood of an enterprise. You must preserve existing sources of income. You only look for new markets to conquer when your current base is secure.

Successful advances are like climbing a ladder. You gradually shift your weight from one rung to the next. The rule is that you move into new markets quickly, but you abandon old bases slowly. In emergencies, you can be forced to move because your existing position has fallen apart, but normally you preserve your existing sources of revenue as you advance.

If your existing business is not very profitable, you have to work more carefully. If moving into new markets hollows out your existing position, such a move can be fatal. In this situation, you focus less on external opportunities in the market and more on internal opportunities in your systems. You need less strategy and more planning. Instead of looking for openings in the market, you look for openings within your systems to control your expenses. As your systems improve, you eventually have more resources than you need to preserve your existing revenue stream. This is when you move into new opportunities in the marketplace.

Many businesses get this process backward. When their existing businesses are doing well, they devote their EXCESS

RESOURCES to internal systems, but they neglect pursuing new opportunities. They wait until their existing businesses are in trouble before considering new opportunities. Putting more resources into profitable operations can be necessary to support growth, but frequently you are working at the wrong end of the law of diminishing returns. For every additional dollar you put in, you are going to get less and less of a return.

People tend to let necessity dictate their attempts at advance. For example, people look for a new job at the worst possible time: when they are out of work. You are much more successful if you counter this tendency. It is a hundred times easier to find a new job when you are doing well in your existing job. It is also a hundred times easier to pursue new opportunities when your existing business is doing well.

New opportunities are more plentiful than most people think, but the best opportunities do not come on any schedule. Because of this, you must protect and build up your existing business and wait patiently until a new opportunity appears. When a new opportunity appears, you must let your existing business take care of itself while you concentrate on your advance.

Remember:

- ✖ You do not pursue opportunities unless your existing position is secure.
- ✖ You do not pursue an opportunity unless you have an excess of resources.
- ✖ You do not pursue an opportunity unless t meets the requirements of the Observe Opportunities Formula.

2. Avoid Direct Competition

How can I fight with my competitors for market control?

You never fight COMPETITORS IN THE MARKET directly or try to control the market. The marketplace is bigger than both you and your competitors. There are right ways and wrong ways to deal with the competition. The worst approach is to target a competitor's strong points.

The most common strategic mistake is to simply copy competitors who already dominate a market. Imitation works in specific competitive situations that we cover later, but the success of your competitors in a market never defines an opportunity.

What happens when you directly attack established competitors? You discover that you cannot make their market position your own. You can try to duplicate their systems and contacts. You can try to offer a product that is superior in every way. You still won't win their customers. This seems unfair, but it is the way it is. You can't let this frustrate and anger you. You can't change it by wasting money on marketing. All competitors must create their own unique positions. Trying to destroy the positions of others is a disaster.

People naturally follow the crowd. This is especially true in business, where every business tries to copy the latest popular product or idea. This never works because crowded markets are unprofitable markets. Following the crowd to find an opportunity is like searching for the pot of gold at the end of the rainbow.

If you want to be successful, go after empty market spaces—openings—not markets that are already crowded. You must see openings in the market and fill them before competitors recognize them. The power of this formula is that it moves you away from conflict with competitors. It moves you into areas where you can win away their business without fighting them. It puts you in control because you are always picking your own customers.

Your competitors can be well entrenched in their markets. You cannot beat them by going after their markets directly, in the same way that they do. Even though you share your market neighborhood with them, you must see the space differently than they do. You don't look at what competitors are doing. You look at what they are failing to do.

You don't want to fight your competitors for customers. Battling over customers is never profitable, even if you win them. I guarantee that no matter how dominant your competitors are, some of their customers are unhappy. This is certain because no one can do everything well. When you recognize this unhappiness and its cause, you are well on the path to finding your opportunity.

Remember:

- ✖ Your competitors' success does not define an opportunity.
- ✖ Never go after markets where competitors are entrenched.
- ✖ Never fight for customers because it is unprofitable.

3. Use Competitors' Size Against Them

What if my competitors already have all my potential customers?

The bigger the company, the more certain it is that they have unhappy customers. You must focus on the customers that competitors have served the most poorly, the needs that they leave unsatisfied. Customers choose you because you have first chosen them. When you choose to target a group of customers, you choose to fill a particular type of need. The larger your competitors are, the more customers they are trying to satisfy and the more specific needs they must neglect.

Competitors may be bigger, but if they are focused on satisfying their average customer, how can their size hurt you? Most customers are not average. The larger their customer base, the more customers fall outside the "average" range.

You beat competitors, no matter how large, by choosing where and when you compete. Markets that seem difficult are really easy when you understand the power of choice. Your choices control how much competition you have. You can divide the market regions to define where you compete best. You can fulfill the customers' needs that competitors do not address.

Some competitors will always be much bigger than you are, but this means that they have many areas in which they can invest their resources. You *want* them to spread themselves too thin. You can then choose the opening that you want to address. You target customers who are well suited to your mission and skills. You choose customers whom your opponent has ignored because their needs are poorly suited to your competitor's mission and skill.

If competitors work globally, you focus locally. If they offer mass-market products, you can offer customized ones. If they deal in large volumes, you can offer limited release. If they use standard terms, you can create special ones. The list goes on and on.

Your much larger, richer, more professional, more experienced competitors will continually overlook opportunities that are right under their noses. How can they hit a target that they cannot see?

You control where you compete. They cannot control you.

Remember:

- ⊗ In a free market, you choose what you do.
- ⊗ You use your choices to control competitors.
- ⊗ This means that you can see what they are bad at.

4. Leverage Competitors' Strengths Against Them

How can I compete when my competitors are not only bigger but have many more strengths than I do?

Strategy teaches that strength is the source of weakness. Only by studying the KNOWN STRENGTHS OF COMPETITORS can you see where they are leaving opportunities. You must see how to put your strengths against your competitors' weaknesses.

Your competitors can have all types of different strengths. It doesn't matter what those strengths are. Like every organization, they cannot do everything well. They have to choose where to focus their resources. When they choose what strengths to develop, they are also choosing to develop a weakness.

Strength and weakness are another pair of those complementary opposites. Strength and weakness are two sides of the same condition. You discover opponents' weaknesses by studying their strengths.

This is simpler than it may sound at first.

If your competitors focus on price, they must sacrifice some aspect of quality. If they focus on high quality, they are vulnerable on price. If they focus on doing specific things extremely well, they perform a broad range of services poorly. If they focus on a broad range of services, they lose the ability to perfect any one of those services. If they emphasize standards and speed, they must de-emphasize customization and personal service.

Whatever competitors do well, they are leaving an opening for you to do the opposite. Instead of envying their strengths, you can turn those strengths into weaknesses. Their packaging is more professional? Aim for a more natural look. Everyone knows who they are? Emphasize that only the select few know to work with you. If competitors attempt everything, they will do everything poorly and they will leave openings everywhere.

The truth is that human needs and tastes are infinite. All customers have unmet needs. Solving one set of needs creates another. You pick your opportunities to address unmet needs. All competitors offer specific solutions. They cannot satisfy every customer.

Remember:

- ⊠ Study your competitors' strengths, not weaknesses.
- ⊠ Turn their apparent strengths into weaknesses.
- ⊠ There are always an infinite number of unmet needs.

5. Keep Your Focus a Secret

What will stop my competitors from addressing the same problems that I want to target?

If you target competitors' strengths, you work their blind spots. If you target obvious weaknesses, your competitors are already working on these problems. Your competitors must not recognize the opening that you see as an opportunity. You don't want to tackle problems that they plan to

address. You want to tackle problems that they cannot plan to address. These openings arise from their strengths, not their weaknesses.

You must keep your desire to leverage their strengths against them a secret. You don't want them to recognize their strengths as weaknesses. Don't give your competitors any ideas. They will be confident in their strengths if you don't draw their attention.

As you move toward these markets, do it quietly without competitors noticing. Do not let your competitors know what you are up to. Keep quiet about what you are doing. Make sales quietly. Avoid the media. Communicate to customers directly so your competitors can't react.

Remember:

- Competitors cannot see their strengths as weaknesses.
- You must secretly redefine the market.
- They can easily counter you if they see what you are doing.

6. Focus Where Competitors Cannot

You want to be assured that your competitors are too distracted to care about holding the customers you target. You also don't want them trying to win those customers back before you make them yours. This means that you have to know where competitors are planning to move in the future. You should know what new products they are developing and in which markets they plan to expand.

The new plans divert competitors' limited attention from their existing customers. Where competitors divide their attention, they create openings. If you know where they are expanding, you also know who they are forgetting. Focus your venture on gaps in their attention.

When you focus on a small group of customers, you concentrate your resources. You must focus all your efforts into areas competitors serve poorly. You can then put a lot of resources into areas where others have put few. You can easily do a better job there than your much larger competitors.

Remember:

- ✖ Know what competitors are planning for the future.
- ✖ This tells you which customers they are neglecting.
- ✖ You can then focus your attention on these customers.

7. Match Your Resources

Why should I want my competitors' problem customers?

Your competitors, problem customers are not your problem customers. People tend to avoid problems, especially other people's problems, but your competitors' problems are not your problems. A precious few of your competitors' problems are your opportunities.

Problems are created by unsatisfied needs. Unsatisfied needs are openings. They are the true emptiness that creates opportunities. Every one of those needs points to an opening, an opportunity. To be skilled in finding opportunities, you must search out problems that others have left unresolved.

We all know that success come from satisfying people's needs, but we still don't recognize the opportunities hidden in every problem. Just like people thoughtlessly miss opportunities by following the crowd, most people miss opportunities by avoiding problems.

How can you tell if a competitor's problem is your opportunity? You have to consider how well those unmet needs match your MISSION, your resources, and your time constraints. Competitors leave gaps in the market because they cannot do everything well. However, you cannot do everything well either. You want to aggressively fill the gaps that competitors leave when those gaps fit your own resources.

Every opportunity you reject frees you to pursue a better opportunity down the road.

You must be selective about what opportunities you pursue. You want to ask yourself three questions. Does satisfying these unmet needs meet your business mission? How well does the problem space match your resources? Will you solve the problem first?

You develop a mission to help you select the opportunities. If you are true to your mission, you will become better and better at solving a particular kind of problems.

RESOURCE FIT combines your enterprise's skills with your excess capacity. Your enterprise must have the right amount of excess resources to address the size of the market. The type of barriers blocking the opening must be well suited to your personal skills and your enterprise's systems. You must be able to easily contact the market and provide it a solution. If you cannot do both, the resource fit is not right.

Your affinity and proximity to the problem must give you a FIRST-MOVER ADVANTAGE. The best preparation for winning a market position is getting to the market first. In some market spaces, this is the single most important issue.

If you get to a market first, then you have time to build up your position and lay traps for your competitors. Since they are playing catch-up, it is easy to exhaust your new competitors. You can drain rich competitors. You can even push around bigger competitors. Didn't I say that strategy was fun?

Learn from the history of successful ventures. Success goes to those who make progress easy. Your ideal customer is one who is inexpensive to win. You don't have to become famous to win new markets. You also don't have to take chances in winning customers.

You must engage only in successful campaigns. Sell to markets that you can easily satisfy. Never pass by an opening that makes competitors look bad.

Remember:

- Some competitors' problems are your opportunities.
- Problems must fit your mission and resources.
- You need the first-mover advantage of position.

8. Be Patient in Waiting for Opportunities

If an opportunity doesn't really play to my strengths, can I develop new skills to take advantage of it?

If you cannot see an opening that clearly fit your abilities, you must not move. You cannot always find a new opportunity. They may be there, but if you don't see them, be patient. You will eventually discover new opportunities. Then you can advance.

You must only go after markets that you are sure you can win. Avoid markets that are too large for you to dominate. Go after markets that are small enough for you to satisfy completely. You must have the resources to campaign for these customers. Go after a market when you have an easy solution to the problem. Avoid crowded markets. Look for markets where you have a FIRST MOV-

ER ADVANTAGE. Until then, you must conserve your resources so that you have plenty of ammunition when the right opportunity appears.

Strategy is the lazy person's road to success. Working smart means avoiding what is hard!

You may see new customers that you would like to win. However, you may not see an afford-able solution for those customers. This means the opportunity isn't quite right. You may see how to win new customers by spending a lot of money. This also shows that the problem is not an opportunity.

You want to move into new markets effortlessly. You must avoid risking your current customers. Wait for the right time to move. Don't try to be too clever. Learning about potential opportunities is easy if you listen to your contact network. Don't imagine opportunities where you want them.

Success only requires enough faith to believe that people have an endless supply of problems. You will eventually observe opportunities that you can win without effort. Avoid highly competitive situations. Invest resources only if it is clear that a market can be profitable. You will succeed if you avoid making hasty decisions.

You build a great business by first finding the right customers. Only then do you worry about investing resources. Find the right customers for your business and then invest only in what you absolutely need to win them.

Remember:

- You must wait and be very selective.
- You must not imagine you can meet needs that you can't.

✖ The right opportunities are always obvious.

Final Thoughts on Observing Opportunities

⊖ Analyze your position and learn about your strengths and weaknesses. Look to advance your position by knowing what needs to be done and what does not need to be done. When you pick a group of customers, know which people are satisfied and which people have needs. When you choose to compete, know where you have the advantage and where you are overmatched.

⊖ Use your existing competitive position as the basis for advancing your position. You must defend your position and move into new market spaces when ready. You want to keep potential customers and competitors guessing.

⊖ Commit to opportunities where your strengths meet competitors' weaknesses. Work where your competitors are ignorant. Competitors should only learn about your enterprise when you have won away customers. Competitors should not understand how your position is winning customers.

⊖ You find real success by making it easy. If you don't understand the forces shaping the winners and losers in business, you cannot harness those forces. If you fight the dynamics of the marketplace, you are doomed to fail.

⊖ You alone determine your success or failure. Creating a successful position is a matter of being the best in one area rather than the second best in another. Creating a losing market position is a matter of making poor market choices.

Learn More About The Observe Opportunities Formula

This chapter has been expanded into the third volume of a nine-volume work on strategy called Sun Tzu's Playbook. *The articles in this volume are listed below.*

3.0.0 Identifying Opportunities: Sun Tzu's five keys to understanding the use of opportunities to advance a position.

3.1 Strategic Economics: Sun Tzu's six keys to balancing the cost and benefits of positioning.

3.1.1 Resource Limitations: Sun Tzu's six keys to understanding the inherent limitation of strategic resources.

3.1.2 Strategic Profitability: Sun Tzu's nine keys to understanding gains and losses.

3.1.3 Conflict Cost: Sun Tzu's six keys to the costly nature of resolving competitive comparisons by conflict.

3.1.4 Openings: Sun Tzu's seven keys to seeking openings avoids costly conflict.

3.1.5 Unpredictable Value: Seven keys to understanding the limitations of predicting the value of positions.

3.1.6 Time Limitations: Sun Tzu nine keys to understanding the time limits on opportunities.

3.2 Opportunity Creation: Five keys to understanding how change creates opportunities.

3.2.1 Environmental Dominance: Sun Tzu's five keys to seeing why openings must be created by others.

3.2.2 Opportunity Invisibility: Sun Tzu five keys to seeing why opportunities are always hidden.

3.2.3 Complementary Opposites: Five keys to understanding the dynamics of balance from opposing forces.

3.2.4 Emptiness and Fullness: Sun Tzu's nine keys to the transformations between emptiness and fullness.

3.2.5 Dynamic Reversal: Sun Tzu's five keys to understanding how situations reverse themselves naturally.

3.2.6 Opening Matrix Tool: Six keys to building a matrix to help us identify unseen openings using Sun Tzu's five elements of positioning.

3.3 Opportunity Resources: Eight keys to understanding the nature of the excess resources needed to fill openings.

3.4 Dis-Economies of Scale: Sun Tzu's six keys to seeing opportunities are created by the size of others.

3.4.1 Unity Breakdown: Sun Tzu's eight keys to understanding the opposition of size and unity.

3.4.2 Opportunity Fitness: Sun Tzu's seven keys to understanding the problems for large organization finding new opportunities that fit their size.

3.4.3 Reaction Lag: Sun Tzu's six keys to understanding why organizations react slower as they grow larger.

3.5 Strength and Weakness: Six keys to seeing how opportunities are created by the strength of others.

3.6 Leveraging Subjectivity: Sun Tzu's seven keys to understanding openings between subjective and objective positions.

3.7 Redefining the Comparison: Sun Tzu's eight keys to redefining a competitive arena to create relative mismatches.

3.8 Strategic Matrix Analysis: Four keys to understanding two-dimensional representations of strategic space.

—FORMULA 4—
RECOGNIZE RESTRICTIONS

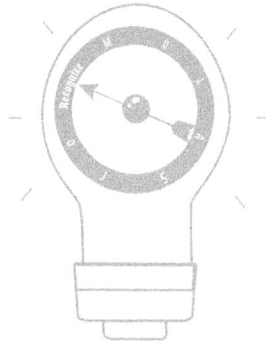

Places for Advancing and Defending

You cannot pursue every opportunity you discover. You must be selective. Opportunities represent potential positions. Each position has its own unique character. Each has its own limitations. These restrictions determine how easily a position can be defended and advanced. You must consider the restrictions in your current and future position before you make a change.

You must understand a position's potential as a stepping-stone to future positions. The Recognize Restrictions Formula teaches you to evaluate the potential and limitations hidden in every competitive position. You cannot invest in positions that are difficult to defend. You cannot move into positions that are dead ends.

Different Positions, Different Restrictions

Why should I care about the restrictions of my current or future position?

Competitive positions are stepping-stones. You are always trying to use your current position to move to a new and better position. You must be able to defend your existing position long enough to move to another one. How easily you can defend your position and eventually move to a better position is determined by the shape of its market space. Some positions are easy to defend; others are more difficult. Some positions are difficult to advance while others make advancing easy.

Competitive positions occupy market space. Business texts discuss markets in terms of segments or niches. These terms describe the limits of a market. In strategy, we prefer the term *market space*. We are less concerned with the boundaries of market spaces than we are with their form. The shape of these market spaces determines how easily positions are defended and advanced.

The most important region to understand is the space between people's ears.

Market spaces exist both in physical space and mind space. Your business has a physical location. Its location describes its physical relationships with customers, competitors, and suppliers. Your business also has a psychological location. Its psychological position maps how your customers, competitors, and supplliers position you in their mental image of the marketplace.

As we move deeper into the information age, physical market space is becoming less important while psychological or mental space is becoming more important. Affinity trumps proximity. Advances in transportation and communication make physical proximity less important. The growing access of customers to a wider variety of product alternatives makes psychological affinity more important. Physical location is still important for retailers, but psychological position is of growing importance to every type of business, including retail, because of the range of choices available.

All spaces have shape. Physical spaces have shape. Psychological spaces have shape. Market spaces, a combination of both, have shape. Though it is easier to discuss shape in physical terms, the most important forces shaping markets today are psychological. Your success depends more upon customers' perceptions than upon physical location. It doesn't matter how physically close customer are if you are psychologically remote.

It is easier to see a position's restrictions if you think in terms of its form and shape.

Because it exists primarily in people's minds, market space is subjective. Each customer and competitor defines it a little differently. Your position within a market space is both subjective and relative. It is defined only by how people mentally compare you with your competitors. This formula enables you to transform subjective, relative market positions into concrete decisions about market potential.

To see the potential in any competitive position, you must first understand its shape and form in psychological space.

The Recognize Restrictions Formula

INGREDIENTS:

1) Area, 2) barriers, 3) challenges, 4) confined regions, 5) spread-out regions, 6) barricaded regions, 7) wide-open regions, 8) fragile regions, 9) optimal regions, 10) self-destructive enterprises, 11) overextended enterprises, 12) distracted enterprises, 13) inefficient enterprises, 14) undisciplined enterprises.

INSTRUCTIONS:

1) See competitive positions in terms of three dimensions. 2) Compare positions to the six benchmark regions to understand their restrictions. 3) Evaluate the internal imbalances of the enterprises in your competitive neighborhood. 4) Analyze the restrictions of market spaces and limitations of organizations before moving out of or into a new position.

Remember:

⊗   Markets exists both in physical space and mental space.

⊗   All market positions have shape and form within space.

⊗   The form of your position determines its potential.

1. See the Dimensions of Market Space

How can I envision the shape of market space?

Like physical space, the psychological space of the market also has three dimensions. These dimensions are area, obstacles, and challenges. These terms have very specific meanings in the science of strategy.

AREA measures the range of psychological territory that a market covers. A market can address a small number of needs for a small group of people. Such a market position covers a very small market area. A market can also address a wide variety of needs for a large group of people. Then the market position covers a large market area. The more area in a market space, the more difficult that space is to defend.

BARRIERS refer to the number of problems you encounter in moving from one market space to another. Think of these problems or obstacles as "barriers to entry." The more barriers in a market space, the more time, effort, or resources it takes to navigate that space. A market space that is easy to get into has few barriers to entry. A market space that is difficult to get into has many barriers to entry. The more barriers in a market space, the easier it is to defend but the harder it is to advance into it.

CHALLENGES refers to the type of risks you encounter as you move out of certain types of market spaces. Some market spaces are challenging because you cannot leave them without weakening your position. Other market spaces are challenging because if you attempt to leave them, you destroy them and cannot return to them. Both challenges make advances difficult.

Remember:

- Market space area creates problems for defense.
- Market space barriers make defense easy and advance difficult.
- Market space challenges make advance difficult.

2. Compare Positions to Six Extremes

How can I easily compare positions in terms of these three dimensions?

There are no absolutes in strategy. Everything is relative. Comparing your position to that of your competitors is too complicated for market space. You have three dimensions and a lot of competitors. You could graph it all out. Consultants love that stuff. They charge. But there is an easier way. You can gauge the potential of a given competitive position by comparing it to the six extreme variations of the three dimension. We call these extremes the six benchmarks.

You examine positions one dimension at a time. For area, you compare your position to the smallest market area and largest market area. For barriers, you compare your positions to positions with the most market barriers and the fewest. For challenges, you compare positions to the challenges of market niches and market peaks. By examining each of these six benchmark regions one at a time, you get a sense of the restrictions of any given market position.

CONFINED regions occupy a very limited market relative to the size of your company. You get the potential out of these spaces if you establish your position before your competitors do. These markets are potentially easy to defend if you satisfy customer demand. If you do not satisfy all the demand within these markets, you can be attacked by competitors who can enter these markets simply by copying your efforts.

Confined market spaces are easy to get into if you discover them before the competition. They are easy to defend if you take care of your customers. Their only restriction is that they offer no room for expansion. To advance your position, you must move into new markets, ideally market spaces that are related.

SPREAD-OUT regions are very large markets relative to the size of your company. These opportunities are too big for your enterprise. They spread your limited resources too thinly across too large of a market area. You waste your efforts on these market spaces. You cannot defend against competitors within them.

Spread-out market spaces look like they have great potential. The truth is that spread-out market positions are inherently weak. You want to identify competitors that have spread-out positions and move into special segments of

their markets. It is easy to win customers from companies with spread-out positions.

BARRICADED regions occupy market spaces that have many barriers to entry. These positions are easy to protect. You realize the potential of these market spaces by establishing yourself in them before competitors do. You must then make sure all potential customers are aware of your position before any competition makes its way into the market. If you win a dominant position in these markets first, you can only lose that position to competitors if you abandon it.

Barricaded positions are difficult to get into but easy to defend. You can protect barricaded positions even in markets that are relatively larger that your enterprise. You can grow easily within a barricaded positions as long as you work behind walls, keeping barriers to entry between you and your competitors.

WIDE-OPEN regions exist within market spaces with no barriers to entry. You can get into these positions easily. The problem is that competitors can come into these market spaces at any time. These ventures are difficult to defend. It helps if you get into them first and become well known.

If you are in a wide-open position, you always have to be concerned about making a profit in these markets. The threat of new competition coming into the market tends to depress prices and margins. If you can win the most dedicated and profitable customers in these markets, you can make money in these market spaces.

FRAGILE regions are niches that pigeonhole you in a challenging market space. Fragile market positions rely on a commitment to your customers to offer a specific product in a specific way. It is like a marriage between an enterprise and its customers. If you try to advance your position by selling to new customers in a different way, it is like filing for divorce. Once broken, the trust on which these positions are built is destroyed. For example, if a company that distributors to retailers starts opening its own retail stores, it ends its wholesale business by competing with its customers.

Fragile positions are easy to get into and easy to defend, but they are difficult to advance. If you try to advance and fail to establish your new position, you cannot return to the safety of your old niche. You destroy these positions when you try to move out of them. Fragile positions are challenging because your advance to a new position must succeed the first time. If your move to a new position fails, you put yourself out of business.

OPTIMAL regions are like the mountain peaks. You cannot move away from these peaks without going downhill. There are no better positions anywhere around these market positions. They are the strongest possible positions in the market space.

When you are in optimal positions, you can only advance by growing the market space. You cannot let yourself get enticed away. You cannot take optimal positions for granted in challenging markets. This was the mistake that Coke made when it tried to replace its traditional formula with New Coke.

You can see the restrictions in your own market position by comparing it to each of these six benchmark regions. You must understand your market space in terms of its area, barriers, and challenges. A market space cannot be, at the same time, both confined and spread out since these are both opposite extremes of market area. However, a market space can be confined and barricaded and fragile.

To understand the shape of your market position, you only need to ask yourself three questions.

How confined or spread out is your market position?

How barricaded or wide open is your market position?

How fragile or optimal is your market position?

Once you understand the shape of your market position in terms of the six benchmark regions, the formula will tell you how easily your position will be to establish, defend, and advance. You will also know how you must utilize that particular type of space.

Remember:

- Confined positions are easy to defend.
- Spread-out positions are hard to defend.
- Barricaded positions are easy to defend but hard to advance.
- Wide-open positions are hard to defend but easy to advance.
- Fragile positions are destroyed when you try to advance.
- Optimal positions can only be weakened.

3. Evaluate Imbalances in the Enterprise

Doesn't the condition of my organization also have an impact on a position's potential?

To understand your options, you have to consider the effect of restrictions on the enterprise. Certain restrictions expose certain weaknesses in an enterprise. The six flaws of organizations are amplified by the restrictions in the six benchmark regions. You can diagnose these weaknesses to predict how a given organization will respond to the restrictions of a market space.

Six weaknesses can handicap any organization. They affect both your own enterprise and your competitors' enterprises. The presence of these flaws makes it difficult for any organization to take advantage of any market space. However, each of these handicaps is exaggerated by one particular set of restrictions.

SELF-DESTRUCTIVE enterprises result from a lack of mission. Their problems are most apparent in confined regions.

To take advantage of a confined market space, an organization must be united. When an organization is not united, its people follow their own personal goals. They want to run their operations independently. These organizations cannot focus on their mission. This means that these enterprises will self-destruct over time. This is especially true in a confined position where internal unity is critical.

OVEREXTENDED enterprises have to pull back from their market position. Their greatest weakness is spread-out regions.

A spread-out market space looks inviting because the market's potential seems so much larger than the enterprise. This is an illusion. This thinking fails to consider the competition. When an organization is spread out in a large market space, competitors can focus on one segment of that market. They can put superior resources against resources that are spread too thinly. Competition forces enterprises in spread-out market positions to pull back.

DISTRACTED enterprises suffer from self-satisfied leadership. They have the most problems in barricaded regions.

Barricaded positions are easy to defend but they require concentration. The safety of a barricaded position allows leadership to become lazy and sloppy. Protected from competition, an organization's systems decay, becoming inconsistent and undependable. Their operations become more costly. Their lack of focus makes virtually all monopolies noncompetitive over time.

INEFFICIENT enterprises waste their resources. They have the most difficulty in wide-open regions.

Wide-open market positions invite competition. Prices are pressured in markets with few barriers to entry. An organization must make the best possible use of its resources. The competitor that makes the best possible use of its resources still makes a profit at the lowest price. In a wide-open market, organizations that are too inefficient do not survive.

UNDISCIPLINED enterprises require not only good leadership judgment, but leadership control over the organization. They are most vulnerable in fragile regions.

Fragile market positions require discipline. An enterprise can have very efficient systems, but to escape from the challenge of a niche market, the leadership must know where it has to stay in its market and when it is safe to advance to one with more potential. Some organizations are too undisciplined to survive the restrictions of these market spaces.

UNTRAINED enterprises have poor systems. They have the most problems in optimal regions.

Optimal market positions require minimal decision-making on the part of the enterprise's leadership. However, they do require good execution by the organization's systems. Poor operations can cause an organization to fall down from the peak of an optimal market position.

The potential of a given market position arises as an interaction between the form of its market space and the weaknesses of the enterprise. An organization can be understood in terms of the relative strength of it leadership, its systems, and the focus and unity it gets from its mission. If you analyze your enterprise and your competitors' enterprises, you are able to predict their options for defending or advancing their positions.

Remember:

- Self-destructive enterprises fall apart in confined regions.
- Overextended enterprises must pull back in spread-out regions.
- Distracted enterprises lose focus in barricaded regions.
- Inefficient enterprises are too wasteful for wide-open regions.
- Undisciplined enterprises are too uncontrolled for fragile regions.
- Untrained enterprises fall down from optimal regions.

4. Determine Potential Before Moving

How do competitors affect the potential in my position?

You must understand the potential of your position before moving into or out of a new position. You must understand how to use market area, market barriers, and market challenges in order to advance your current position. You don't want to move into positions that make future advances more difficult. Each position must be a stepping-stone. This is the only way to build success over time.

You must shape your enterprise to fit the nature of your market position. You do not have to do everything well in every market. You develop the qualities that are critical in your specific market space. You focus on bringing your resources together in confined spaces, on courageous leadership in spread-out markets, on focus in barricaded markets, on efficient systems in wide-open markets, on disciplined leadership in fragile markets, and on effective systems in peak markets. This is how you are profitable in these various market situations. You must invest based on your understanding of your position.

Misjudging the potential of a position is one way you leave openings for competitors.

You must respond to the mistakes your competitors make. You challenge them directly when they misjudge their market position. Forget your original intentions in the marketplace. You cannot plan for every opportunity. You must go after customers and sales when a competitor's mistakes give you an opportunity.

If you understand the position, you can know when pursuing a new market will be too costly. Spread-out regions look big enough for unlimited expansion, but they result in a mismatch of your resources with market size. Open regions look easy to get into, but you have to have efficient systems to survive in them. You have to have the capital to invest to surmount the barriers to entry in barricaded markets. You must avoid pursuing market spaces that will cost you more than they will ever return.

Your ventures must make money, not just win recognition. Get out of any regions that cannot pay off. Success demands that you make a profit. This is how you build your enterprise. This is how you ensure your success.

- ❋ Know the potential of a region before moving out of or into it.
- ❋ Shape your enterprise to fit your market space.
- ❋ You must respond to mistakes competitors make.

Final Thoughts on Recognizing Restrictions

⊙ Market space has shape and form. The shape of the market space you inhabit determines how easy it will be to defend and expand your market position.

⊙ This formula provides a benchmark for measuring market potential. It offers six benchmark regions that represent the purest forms of extreme, static conditions. This benchmark defines the way in which each of these six market conditions must be utilized.

⊙ Every enterprise has weaknesses and strengths. To make the most of the potential hidden within your position, you must know what elements within your enterprise need to be developed.

⊙ Your ability to harvest market potential determines your future. You may know that your enterprise is ready for the market. You must also know that your competitors are poorly suited for that market. Finally, you must also know exactly how to use your resources in that market space. If you understand your market space and its dynamics, your profits are assured.

More About The Recognize Restrictions Formula

This chapter has been expanded into the fourth volume of a nine-volume work on strategy called Sun Tzu's Playbook. *The articles in this volume are listed below.*

4.0 Leveraging Probability: Sun Tzu's nine principles for making better decisions regarding our choice of opportunities.

4.1 Future Potential: Five keys to understanding the limitations and potential of current and future positions.

4.2 Choosing Non-Action: Sun Tzu's seven keys to choosing between action and non-action.

4.3 Leveraging Form: Sun Tzu's seven keys to knowing how we can leverage the form of a territory.

4.3.1 Tilted Forms: Sun Tzu's six keys to understanding space that is dominated by uneven features.

4.3.2 Fluid Forms: Sun Tzu's six keys to selecting opportunities in fast-changing environments.

4.3.3 Soft Forms: Sun Tzu's six keys to understanding space that is dominated by non-supporting features.

4.3.4 Neutral Forms: Sun Tzu's seven keys to evaluating opportunities with no dominant ground form.

4.4 Strategic Distance: Sun Tzu's nine keys to understanding relative proximity in strategic space.

4.4.1 Physical Distance: Sun Tzu's six keys to understanding the issues of proximity in physical space.

4.4.2 Intellectual Distance: Sun Tzu's six keys to understanding the challenges of moving through intellectual space.

4.5 Opportunity Surfaces: Sun Tzu's six keys to judging potential opportunities from a distance.

4.5.1 Surface Area: Sun Tzu's seven keys to choosing opportunities on the basis of their size.

4.5.2 Surface Barriers: Seven keys to understanding how to select opportunities by evaluating obstacles.

4.5.3 Surface Holding Power: Sun Tzu's seven keys to understanding sticky and slippery situations.

4.6 Six Benchmarks: Five keys to understanding simplifying the comparisons of opportunities.

4.6.1 Spread-Out Conditions: Sun Tzu's five keys to recognizing opportunities that are too large.

4.6.2 Constricted Conditions: Sun Tzu's five keys to identifying and using constricted positions.

4.6.3 Barricaded Conditions: Sun Tzu's seven keys to understanding the issues related to the extremes of obstacles.

4.6.4 Wide-Open Conditions: Six keys to understanding the issues related to an absence of barriers.

4.6.5 Fixed Conditions: Sun Tzu's nine keys to understanding positions with extreme holding power.

4.6.6 Sensitive Conditions: Six keys to understanding the affects of positions with no holding power on pursuing opportunities.

4.7 Competitive Weakness: Sun Tzu's six keys to knowing how certain opportunities can bring out our weaknesses.

4.7.1 Command Weaknesses: Sun Tzu's ten keys to the character flaws of leaders and how to exploit them.

4.7.2 Group Weaknesses: Sun Tzu's six keys to understanding organizational weakness and where they fail.

4.8 Climate Support: Sun Tzu's eight keys to choosing new positions based on future changes.

4.9 Opportunity Mapping: Five keys to understanding a two-dimensional tool for comparing opportunities probabilities.

—FORMULA 5—
MINIMIZE MISTAKES

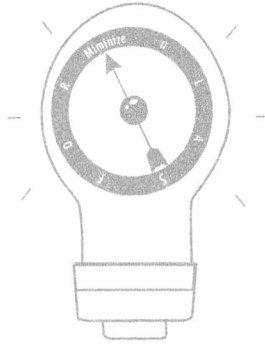

Make Competitive Advances Safely

After you have determined that restrictions don't prevent you from pursuing an opportunity, you must consider the safest way to exploit an opening. Though we learn more from our mistakes than our successes, we must design new ventures so any mistakes don't damage our current position.

Here is the dilemma. All new ventures fail if we pursue them with half measures. However, even if we pursue new ventures wholeheartedly, many will still fail. How do we make sure that those failures don't damage the future of our enterprise? That is why we need the Minimize Mistakes Formula to test your ideas. It minimizes your risk and the impact of failure. It also dramatically increases the eventual certainty of success.

The Limits of Planning

Don't I increase my chances of success if I spend more time and effort planning my move?

Successful competition requires knowing what you can control and what you cannot control. This is a dollars and cents issue. To improve your position, a new venture must be profitable. If you knew which new ventures were going to be profitable, there would be no need for this formula. The truth is that you cannot know how much income a new venture can generate. You cannot know how long or how much it will cost to get going. Therefore, you control what you can.

Competitive environments are dynamic. Within them, people's plans collide continually, creating situations that no one planned. You cannot predict competitive conditions. This limits traditional planning. When you plan, you make decisions in advance. You try to save money and eliminate mistakes by planning. However, in dynamic markets, it is often cheaper and safer to get into the market in a small way and then react to what happens.

When a venture is unproven, no one knows what will happen. People's opinions differ. You plans are based upon what you think will happen, but others can always offer legitimate alternatives. The longer you try to perfect your plans, the more expensive your new venture becomes. While you are busy planning, your new venture cannot get off the ground.

Instead of planning, you want to start testing. You want to get a new venture off the ground as soon as possible. Inertia destroys enthusiasm for any new project. Planning

There are only two kinds of businesses: those that prefer planning over testing and those that make money.

long, careful, drawn-out campaigns for new markets drains your limited resources. These campaigns are more likely to fail. Bigger experiments are never better experiments.

People think that the more detailed the plan, the safer a new venture is. The opposite is true. Planning is meaningless without testing your plans. The desire to keep planning creates a sluggish organization. The longer you plan, the more money you spend. While you are planning, your competitors can test their ideas to see what works. It doesn't matter how smart you think you are. You can't get ahead by falling behind your competitors.

You can sometimes go into a new venture too quickly, but you can never start testing too soon. No successful venture is planned in detail beforehand. You can continue to plan or your can start testing your venture to see what happens. You can't do both at once.

So, what can you realistically plan when undertaking a new venture? You can run a small test.

The Minimize Mistakes Formula

INGREDIENTS:

1) Current activities, 2) a target opportunity, 3) a proven desire, 4) a clear mission, 5) resources to invest

INSTRUCTIONS:

1) Use your current profitability as a guide to expansion by doing less, not more. 2) Identify what you can sell that people are already buying. 3) Root out internal conflict within the organization. 4) Minimize your initial investment. 5) Experiment locally. 6) Create a local competitive mismatch through focus.

Remember:

- Every new venture is more expensive than expected.
- The longer you plan, the less successful you will be.
- Moving quickly with focus works better than planning.

1. Do Less, Not More

How can I be certain that the new venture won't undermine any part of my existing business?

The goal is to improve your competitive position. The strongest competitive positions are the simplest. This means that the best strategy is to grow your enterprise by doing less, not more. You have to approach every new venture as a way of simplifying your enterprise's CURRENT ACTIVITIES.

When you see a TARGET OPPORTUNITY, you naturally want to pursue it. But businesses that grow too complex are seldom profitable. You want to grow by subtraction. If a new opportunity makes sense, it expands on what you are currently doing. Build your enterprise by focusing more narrowly on what you already do profitably.

A decision to do more must be coupled with a decision to do less. If you want to do more of what is most profitable, you must do less of what is less profitable. To start a new venture, you pull away resources from your least profitable activities. If a new venture expands and is more profitable than what you have been doing, you gradually shift more and more resources away from what you have been doing less profitably.

Let me give you an example from my personal experience of how you grow your business by making it simpler.

When we started our software company, we started as general consultants. Our most profitable jobs came from database development, so we slowly stopped doing other projects. By focusing on database projects, our business doubled. Then our most profitable projects were accounting related, so we focused on those projects. We again doubled in size. Then the most profitable accounting sales came from resellers. So we stopped other sales and doubled again. Then the most profitable sales were from large systems. We stopped selling smaller systems. We doubled again. The we saw that our most profitable sales came from order processing. We stopped selling other types of accounting software and doubled in size again.

In strategy, hitting a smaller target is more certain and safe than hitting a larger one.

We became one of the Inc. 500 fastest-growing companies in America not by doing more and more, but by doing less and less. And we did it without any outside financing or borrowing money because we were always working at what was most profitable.

You use every opportunity to further refine and simplify your business. A focused venture is successful. An unfocused venture fails. Selling one product is easy. Selling many products is hard. A concentrated effort is powerful. A divided effort is weak. Well-defined customers make you successful. A mixed group of customers is costly to serve. Clear-cut goals keep you on track. Confused goals get you nowhere.

The more focused your efforts are, the easier it will be to win competitive battles. Still, winning competitive battles doesn't make you successful. Success comes from avoiding competitive battles. All competitive battles decrease profits. The most profitable businesses are those that have the least competition. You must always focus on the profitability of your enterprise and making new ventures profitable as quickly as possible.

This is the power of focus. This is the power of using your profitability to gauge how much better you are than the competition.

Remember:

- Profitability is a guide to what you should be doing.
- New ventures must allow you to do more of what is the most profitable.
- If you just do more, you will become less profitable; you must couple expansion with subtractions.

2. The Goal Is to Make Money

How can I increase the chances that my experimental venture will be a success?

The proof of any project is making a profit. Before you go into any new venture, you need to know what your product is and how you can sell it profitably. While you cannot plan out your entire campaign, you must have a profitable product to get started. You must avoid ventures in which the product is poorly defined. You must avoid ventures in which you are not sure who will buy the product. You must avoid ventures in which it isn't clear how you will make money selling your product.

Instead, choose opportunities where it is easy to see what you have to sell. Choose ventures where customers are easy to identify. Choose opportunities where you are certain your sales will be profitable. If you have to chose between making sales and making profits, you have to choose profits over sales. A dollar in profits is worth more than a million dollars in unprofitable sales. A dollar from the sale of a profitable product is worth a million dollars of sales in unprofitable products.

What is the easiest way of assuring that a venture is profitable? Go after customers that are already paying money for similar products to someone else. Convincing new customers to invest new money in new products is too difficult and too uncertain. Go after customers who have already have a PROVEN DESIRE. This is why you focus on competitors' weaknesses to identify an opportunity . You know that their unhappy customers are willing to spend money. By taking these customers away from competitors, you make money more quickly. You also discourage your competitors at the same time. Taking customers from competitors is a twofer: you take strength away from your competitors and add to your own.

However, you don't take away customers by getting into price wars with them. Nobody makes a profit in a price war. You challenge competitors by taking away customers that you can serve more easily than they can. You must be able to offer a lower price because you have a big cost advantage.

Concentrate your efforts on the most profitable business. Reward your early customers for trusting you. Advertise and promote your success with early adopters. Choose markets that generate repeat business to avoid high sales and marketing costs.

Remember:

- ❋ The proof of a new venture's success is its profitability.
- ❋ Avoid ventures where the source of profits is unclear.
- ❋ Take existing sales from your competitors.

3. Eliminate Internal Distractions

What if the people involved in a new venture are dedicated, but other parts of my organization have other goals?

You are undertaking a new venture. You are going to be devoting time and resources to it. Those resources are taken from elsewhere in your organization. You cannot predict what will happen in the new venture or how it will affect other parts of your organization. This is naturally going to threaten other people in your enterprise.

People are naturally threatened by change. A new venture is always a threat to more established parts of an organization. Though they don't like change, the people within an organization must realize that undertaking new ventures is the key to the survival of the enterprise as a whole.

You must actively train others in your enterprise to expect and accept new ventures. The established part of your business must support new competitive efforts. Everyone must understand that an enterprise grows more successful when it supports new ventures. An enterprise grows weak when it doesn't see the need for new ventures.

The larger the organization, the more difficulty it has moving into new areas because more people are affected.

Internal conflict and political divisions over what is "fair" can undermine your success in several different ways. Ignorant of the need and nature of real opportunities, people in more established part of the business want to force expansion on their schedule. Ignorant of the dynamic nature of competition, they want to abandon new ventures when they get difficult. We call this hamstringing the new venture.

Most people do not understand that you cannot manage a new venture like you do an established business. They don't understand the need for new ventures and the needs of new ventures. This is why everyone needs a copy of this book.

The confusion between controlled and dynamic environments underlies the conflict between an established enterprise and a new venture. An established enterprise exists in a more controlled and predictable space than a new venture. Existing businesses want to plan new ventures like they do proven operations. They think they can manage a new venture according to the same rules that they use to manage established businesses. The goal of a new enterprise isn't to be predictable but to find some way to survive.

Competitive ventures use a different set of rules than already produc- tive operations.

New ventures require different priorities and are run by different sets of rules. The demands of a fast-changing, dynamic environment can only be met by good strategy. To survive in a dynamic, competitive market, you must play by the rules of competition and customers. You must ignore internal desires.

If you let internal politics fester in your organization, everyone will become confused about your goals. Others will undermine confidence in your leadership. Politics will tear any organization apart and invite challenges from outside competitors. The more promising the potential of your organization, the more dangerous political conflicts become.

Establishing a CLEAR MISSION is critical. It unites the different functions within an organization and focuses it on a shared goal. You must not weaken an enterprise's trust in its focus and purpose.

Your good leadership is essential for success. Good leaders recognize the difference between controlled environments and dynamic markets. Good leaders understand the need for direct priorities in these areas. Good leaders know how to focus their investments on the most important task at hand. A lack of clear priorities destroys your chances of success.

Remember:

- ✖ The whole organization must support new ventures.
- ✖ Internal political divisions create failure from success.
- ✖ Everyone must be emotionally invested in the venture.

4. Minimize the Initial Investment

Won't I increase my chances of success if I spend more money?

You have RESOURCES TO INVEST in a new venture, you are never buying an insurance policy. Business is a game you get to play only as long as you have money. Every dime you spend without generating income brings you a little closer to ending the game. You cannot avoid spending money in a new venture, but you can minimize it.

When a venture is new, you cannot know how much money it will generate. It may be a gold mine. It may not generate a dime. People who plan on making a given amount of money from a new, unproven market are just fooling themselves.

You know for certain that your resources are limited. You know for certain that the money you spend on a new, unproven market must come from other parts of your business that are proven. If you don't minimize investment at the beginning of a venture, you will never make a profit. Unregulated spending leads to more spending.

You must think competitively. You cannot think that you can put more and more money into a new venture until it pays off. Minimize your investment in new assets and inventory. Minimize your investments in hiring.

Instead of investing, think about ways that you can make the venture pay for itself. Look for easy ways to take sales from your competitors. Once you get customers buying, you have more money to develop the market. Even when you get money coming in, invest only in the items that you absolutely need. This is the way you ensure that this new market will be profitable.

Remember:

- ✖ Investing more doesn't insure against failure.
- ✖ The more you spend, the less likely you are to make a profit.
- ✖ Spending less makes a profit more likely.

5. Experiment Locally

Don't I increase my chances of success if I try to cover as much territory as possible?

Better communication and transportation have made the world smaller, but when you are exploring a new market area, it is always best to start as close to home as you can. If your experiment with new products, customers, and programs is successful, it can always be expanded later.

Selling to distant customers is costly in many ways. It is easier initially to offer good value and service if you don't have to work over long distances. It is easier to make a profit if you don't have to pay for shipping and travel. Either you or your customers are going to have to pay these costs. Too many businesses today are "going global," only to discover that most of the money they are making goes to FedEx and UPS.

Travel and shipping are the costs of crossing geographic distance. Learning and marketing are the costs of crossing intellectual distance. Learning about a new market distant from your own is expensive. Educating a new market that doesn't know you or your products is costly. High costs make it more difficult to satisfy customers. The high overhead costs of running a distant operation will make you less competitive than more "local" businesses.

These costs can easily consume all your profit potential.

You want to test a new market close to home. Even new markets can be close to home geographically or intellectually. Ideally, they are both. If the venture proves profitable locally, you can then expand geographically as you increase your efficiency. If a new opportunity is too distant—either physically or intellectually—from what you are currently doing, you cannot afford to explore it.

Remember:

※ The more distance you cover, the higher your costs.

※ It is best to start any new venture close to home.

6. Create Local Competitive Mismatch

What is the easiest way to make certain that my new venture will be a success?

Even though you start small, minimizing the size of your investment, you must be totally committed to the success of your venture. Halfhearted efforts are certain to fail. When you work to minimize your mistakes, the only thing you cannot afford to minimize is the quality of your effort. You must persist in trying everything you can think of to make it work. You start small so you can overload the effort with resources.

The biggest danger in starting small is thinking that it doesn't matter if the venture succeeds or not. Just because you have put a minimum at risk never means you can afford to fail. It may take a hundred small failures to find a huge success, but you will never find that success if you don't put your best efforts into each attempt. In creating the light bulb, Edison failed again and again, but not because he was sloppy and disorganized.

Sure, many of these experiments with new markets will fail. You keep them small because there is a chance of failure. A hundred productive failures teach you more precisely what works. A million sloppy, halfhearted failures get you no closer to your goal.

You minimize failure by creating a local mismatch of resources between you and your direct competitors. You focus on the smallest possible market space so you can put a lot more resources into that market than your competitors. If you have ten times more resources in that little area than they do, you can just go around them. If you have five times more resources, you can overpower them. If you have only twice as many resources in your target market, you need to divide the market into something smaller.

In the end, the overall size of your enterprise and the competitors you face doesn't matter. It is the local mismatch that matters. If you are the same size as your competitors, you can always specialize your product, focusing it more tightly on a specific group of customers. If you are smaller than your competitors, you can easily defend a small segment of the overall market. If you are just a fraction of their size, move from market niche to market niche, creating local mismatches of resources, with those larger competitors not even noticing your business. Small companies are not powerful in comparison to the overall market, but they can move much more quickly than large companies. Large companies cannot address the needs of little niches as quickly as small companies can.

Remember:

⊗   Start on the smallest possible scale.

⊗   Commit everything to creating a small success.

⊗   Create a complete imbalance in focus.

Final Thoughts on Minimizing Mistakes

⊖ Make all your new ventures pay for themselves as quickly as possible. Avoid expensive, slow start-ups that get bogged down in planning. You cannot plan new ventures in the same way you can established businesses. Your knowledge of good strategy is the key to working in a competitive environment. It determines whether or not your organization is manageable. Strategy determines whether or not your new ventures are successful or a threat to your future.

-⊖- Focus on what you can do best. This means balancing your capabilities against those of your competitors. If you do that, you can always survive in the marketplace. You may know your capabilities but not those of your competitors. Then for every successful new venture, another venture will fail. You can be ignorant of your abilities and those of your competitors. Then every new venture is doomed. As an entrepreneur, you must move into new areas. Your commitment to new ventures gives you focus. This focus unites your enterprise without limiting it.

-⊖- You must minimize your mistakes. Success comes from knowing what needs to be done and what you can leave undone. Success comes from focusing your limited resources on new ventures of the appropriate size. Success comes from eliminating problems that others overlook. Success comes from making the organization's mission clear. Success comes from providing leadership and eliminating the internal divisions that interfere with your ability to compete.

More About The Minimize Mistakes Formula

This chapter has been expanded into the fifth volume of a nine-volume work on strategy called Sun Tzu's Playbook. *The articles in this volume are listed below.*

5.0.0 Minimizing Mistakes: Sun Tzu's five general keys to minimizing mistakes in advancing a position.

5.1 Mission Priorities: Sun Tzu's five keys to aligning our actions with mission.

5.1.1 Event Pressure: Sun Tzu's eight keys to knowing how to avoid mistakes under the pressure of events.

5.1.2 Unproductive Responsibility: Sun Tzu's seven keys to knowing how our planned activities develop a life of their own.

5.2 Opportunity Exploration: Sun Tzu's seven keys to understanding a mental framework for exploring opportunities.

5.2.1 Choosing Adaptability: Sun Tzu's five keys to choosing actions that allow us a maximum of future flexibility.

5.2.2 Campaign Methods: Sun Tzu's five keys to understanding the use of campaigns and their methods.

5.2.3 Unplanned Steps: Sun Tzu's seven keys to distinguishing campaign adjustments from steps in a plan.

5.3 Reaction Time: Sun Tzu's five keys to the use of speed in choosing actions.

5.3.1 Speed and Quickness: Sun Tzu's seven keys to understanding the use of pace within a dynamic environment.

5.3.2 Opportunity Windows: Sun Tzu's five keys to the effect of speed upon opposition.

5.3.3 Information Freshness: Sun Tzu's six keys to the choosing actions based on freshness of information.

5.4 Minimizing Action: Sun Tzu's six keys to understanding minimizing waste, i.e. less is more.

5.4.1 Testing Value: Sun Tzu's five keys to choosing actions to test for value.

5.4.2 Successful Mistakes: Six keys to understanding the advantages in learning from our mistakes.

5.5 Focused Power: Sun Tzu's five keys to size consideration in safe experimentation.

5.5.1 Force Size: Sun Tzu's eight keys to limiting the size of force in an advance.

5.5.2 Distance Limitations: Sun Tzu's eight keys to the use of short steps to reach distant goals.

5.5.3 Evaluation Deadlines: Sun Tzu's six keys to setting deadlines for evaluating progress.

5.6 Defensive Advances: Sun Tzu's six keys to balancing defending and advancing positions.

5.6.1 Defense Priority: Seven keys to understanding why defense has first claim on our resources.

5.6.2 Acting Now: Sun Tzu's eight keys to acting on opportunities immediately.

—FORMULA 6—

UNDERCUT
UNCERTAINTY

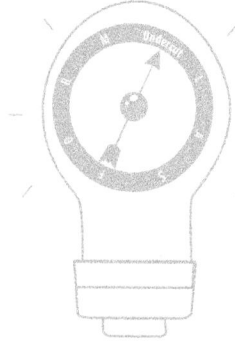

Respond to Changing Conditions

Competitive environments are uncertain. Customers' atti-tudes can change in a moment. Competitors will always do something unexpected. Successful strategies must constantly adjust to these unpredictable conditions. Fortunately, the science of strategy lays out the most common ways situations change and how you should adjust your responses to them. As long as you respond appropriately, you can constantly adapt your methods without being inconsistent in your results.

If you understand the changing situation better than your competitors do, you can use the dynamics of situations to con-trol your opponents' behavior. Markets are unpredictable. If you want to advance your position, you must undercut uncer-tainty by reacting appropriately to changing conditions.

The Power of Choice

If I cannot plan out a new venture, how can I be prepared for what I will meet in a new market?

When you explore an opportunity, you cannot know what exact conditions you will encounter. Not only that, but those conditions will change as your venture continues toward its goal. A competitive campaign is like driving. You know where you want to go, but you have to deal with a wide variety of traffic conditions on the way. You constantly adjust the way you drive to accommodate the traffic.

You cannot succeed in pursuing any opportunity unless you can surmount the challenges you meet along the way. You must be inventive in advancing your position. You must see where situations lead you. You are free to respond appropriately to different situations. Consistent progress requires different adjustments. Every situation offers challenges, but you can always find a good response if you understand the nature of those challenges.

When you go into a new market, you cannot know what you will encounter. You let what you find determine your actions. Successful competitive campaigns do not follow a plan. Different ventures call for different methods at different times. You must be flexible in your responses. You must react quickly to changing conditions. This means you must know exactly how to respond.

You undercut uncertainty by quickly identifying a situation and responding appropriately. Competitive situations may not follow a plan, but they do follow a pattern. As a new venture evolves, it faces a number of common situations. In each situation, something different is required. Sometimes it is speed. Sometimes it is cooperation. Sometimes it is an act of desperation. If you correctly diagnose the situation, you need to know how to respond. If you know how to respond, you will never have to fear uncertainty.

Adapting to situations is the key to success. Many people are unable to recognize their situation. Others recognize their situation, but they do not know how to respond to it. Still others see their situation and know the proper response, but they fail to respond quickly enough. If you are unable to respond effectively, you cannot exploit any opportunity.

The Undercut Uncertainty Formula

INGREDIENTS:

1) The dissipating stage, 2) easy stage, 3) contentious stage, 4) open stage, 5) shared stage, 6) serious stage, 7) difficult stage, 8) limited stage, 9) desperate stage, 9) uneven markets, 10) rapidly changing markets, 11) uncertain markets, 12) solid markets

INSTRUCTIONS:

1) Determine which of the nine common situations or stages you are facing in the competitive market. 2) Immediately adjust your behavior to fit the situation you are in. 3) Control other people's expectations so they will follow you. 4) Recognize and utilize four types of markets. 5) Leverage your values. 6) Know when to take a pause in your campaign.

You must use your resources carefully. Do not assume that competitors will not challenge you. Instead, be ready to meet them. Do not trust that customers won't criticize your company. Instead, you should position your company so that criticize can't easily attack it.

Remember:

- ⊠ You are always free to decide what you will and won't do.
- ⊠ You should let situations dictate your response.
- ⊠ Don't let your character get in the way of your success.

1. Know the Nine Common Stages

If my new ventures are going great one moment and are in trouble the next, what is happening?

Any competitive campaign or new venture passes through certain predictable stages. Early on, you run into dissipating, easy, and contentious situations. Later on, you run into open, shared, and serious situations. Toward the end, situations become more difficult, limited, and, finally, desperate.

Before a new venture even starts, you have to defend against outside threats and criticism. This is the DISSIPATING STAGE.

When you move into a new market, you idea and your enterprise are a novelty. This is the EASY STAGE.

When you start to see some success, competitors and rivals want to get in on it. This is the CONTENTIOUS STAGE.

When you can make quick progress building your position while competitors are also building their businesses, this is the OPEN STAGE.

Over time, you discover that several non-competing companies also sell to your market. If you can develop good partnerships with them, you will succeed in the market. This is the SHARED STAGE.

As the project goes on, your investment to establish your market position gets bigger and bigger. Critics and competitors are sniping at your back. This is the SERIOUS STAGE.

As time passes, you run into problems that slow the venture down. You encounter barriers to making the venture profitable. Unforeseen changes take place. These obstacles are unavoidable in making progress. This is the DIFFICULT STAGE.

Each of the nine situation re- quires knowing and executing the appropriate response.

When a campaign is getting close to the end, you reach a key transition point. During this time, your options are severely limited. Your entire operation is an easy target if competitors know how limited your options are. This is the LIMITED STAGE.

In the end, you can succeed only if you commit all your resources. You must act quickly. Your venture will fail if you delay. This is the final DESPERATE STAGE.

Conditions change continuously. Every change is a new opportunity to make the right decision. If you run into a problem at the beginning of a campaign, you can still succeed in the end. If you are challenged at the end, you will succeed if you started on the right foot. If you are threatened in the middle of a campaign, you succeed by starting well and finishing strong.

Remember:

- All campaigns pass through predictable stages.
- Each of these situations requires a specific response.
- Your success depends on recognizing your situation.

2. Adapt to Change Instantly

Can I really adjust my operations to respond to all these situation correctly?

At each stage, the response is fairly simple. There is nothing new in any of these situations. They have occurred a million times in competition. You should expect them and be prepared to react appropriately when they arise. These situations will not occur in every venture. You cannot predict if or when they will occur. When you recognize one of them, you must concentrate your efforts on the only appropriate response.

You avoid the dissipating stage by distracting critics and competitors by attacking them instead of defending yourself.

During the easy stage, you cannot be satisfied with what is accomplished quickly and you must become even more aggressive.

During the contentious stage, you avoid getting into battles, such as price wars, and avoid competitors as much as possible.

In the open stage, you keep up with your competitors and copy whatever they do.

In the shared stage, you form partnerships, even with competitors.

In the serious stage, you focus on generating income any way you can, even if only for the short term.

In the difficult stage, you keep going, no matter how slow and difficult your progress becomes.

In the limited stage, you must do the unexpected. You must get creative and unpredictable.

In the desperate stage, you bring all your resources to bear as quickly as possible. Succeed or fail as quickly as possible.

The secret to undercutting uncertainty is being disciplined enough to respond correctly. You cannot respond according to how you feel. You must respond according to your situation.

The faster you recognize and respond to these situations, the more certain your success becomes. Knowing the Undercut Uncertainty Formula allows you to develop these quick reflexes. You must respond to these situations automatically. You act on instinct.

You may question your judgment. What if you are wrong? Should you respond instantly when you see yourself in one of these situations or wait to make certain? There is only one answer. You must act! The secret to success is making the right decisions quickly. The longer you delay, the less likely success becomes.

Remember:

- Each of the nine situations has only one correct response.
- The faster you respond, the better the result.
- You don't have time to question your judgment.

3. Control People's Expectations

If I change my behavior suddenly, won't others lose confidence in me?

Done correctly, your responses should create confidence. Competition is always uncertain. You make decisions every day about how to proceed. If you clearly know how to respond to changing conditions, you increase the confidence others have in you.

To lead people, you must welcome challenges. They give you an opportunity to show your confidence in others. People come together when they are challenged. This is a part of sharing a mission. People work together when they are in the same boat during a storm. When people share adversity, one person rescues the other just as naturally as the right hand helps the left.

This requires confident leadership. You must recognize and explain the conditions you are in. You must know how to use each stage correctly. If you demonstrate that you know exactly what you are doing, you make it impossible for people not to trust you.

Put people in teams. People working together are more courageous than any individual. Put your strongest and weakest supporters together. Use the situation to unite the people and offer direction. Lead them confidently through every stage.

You must take each new venture seriously. Making a serious commitment focuses your efforts. Lack of commitment dissipates your resources.

When you leave your established market and first start a new venture, you must lead others. This is a critical stage.

When you discover others that share your goals, you make them your allies. This is the shared stage.

You never have to be perfect. You just have to be better than competitors at predicting the future.

As a project continues, you must prepare people for situations becoming more difficult. All ventures look promising when you first get into them. This is always the easy stage of a new campaign. As time goes on, resources get stretched thin. This is always the serious stage. Eventually, you cannot back out and you have fewer and fewer options. This is the limited stage. A venture's future can come down to coming through a crisis. This is the desperate stage.

These are all worst-case scenarios. The new venture can stabilize and start making money at any point. However, you need to prepare others for what may happen. You cannot eliminate uncertainty. You can only undercut it. When things go correctly, the situation takes care of itself.

Each stage of a campaign requires the appropriate reaction from others. To succeed in the dissipating stage, , you need the commitment of others before a project begins. In the easy stage, you must let others know that you plan to go as far and as fast as you can. In the contentious stage, you use others to create obstacles for your competitors. In the open stage, you must get people to focus on your business, not your competitors. In the shared stage, you must get others to join you as partners. In the serious stage, you need to generate income from people in any way you can. In the difficult stage, you must give everyone a sense that you will not be discouraged. In the limited stage, you must make sure that your competitors do not know that you are vulnerable. In the desperate stage, you must prove yourself by putting an end to the crisis.

You must make other people feel like they are winners. If you show them that you can respond to both blessing and difficulties, they will follow you. People will have no choice but to give you all they have. This is how you win their commitment.

Remember:
- Provide leadership by understanding the conditions.
- Give people what they need in changing conditions.
- People judge you by how well you respond to challenges.

4. Utilize Market Differences

How can I use the different characteristics of markets against my competitors?

Thus far we have been discussing how you adapt to the nine different common competitive situations. These situations are defined primarily by changes in a competitive campaign. However, you must also adapt appropriately to the four main different types of marketplaces in which you can find yourself. There are uneven markets, rapidly changing markets, uncertain markets, and solid markets. Your competitive journey takes you into all four. You must know how to utilize each to your advantage.

UNEVEN MARKET have many small potential customers are dominated by a few very large customers. When large customers but dominate a market, rely on small customers. Establish a visible position with a few larger customers, but never battle with the larger accounts for their business. This is how you grow your business in uneven marketplaces.

RAPIDLY CHANGING MARKET are dominated by technological or organizational transformation. When markets are changing rapidly, avoid them. Wait for your competitors to get embroiled in them. Wait until market changes divide your opponents' resources and then use their division as an opportunity. You don't want to be wrestling with changes yourself when you meet the competition. Get ahead of the market trends and keep yourself visible. Always side with the forces of change in fast-changing markets.

UNCERTAIN MARKETS are dominated by confusion, rumors, and a lack of solid information. These markets have many undependable customers. Get out of these markets as quickly as you can. You may meet competitive challenges under uncertain conditions. When you do, keep the parts of the market you know the best. Protect yourself from getting pushed into more chaotic situations. This is how you meet competitors in uncertain markets.

SOLID MARKETS are the opposite of the other three. They are just right. They are even, stable, and certain. When markets are solid, keep your operations and products flexible. Base your position on the most profitable, visible products. Stay in front of the competition and avoid missteps. This is how you meet competitors in solid markets.

You can use the market topography against your competitors in any of these four markets. You must not treat all market spaces as if they were the same. You must adapt to the unique conditions in the marketplace, just as you adapt to the changing character of your enterprise.

Remember:

⊠   There are four different market topographies.

⊠   You can leverage each one against your competitors.

5. Leverage Your Values

In all these situations, how do I establish that I am different than my competitors?

Your core mission acts as a stabilizing force as your new ventures pass through different stages and take you into different markets. The shared values defined by your mission unite the organization and give it strength. You must know to utilize this mission as you adapt to unexpected changes.

Enterprises are stronger when selling based on values rather than selling on price alone. Your organization is healthier when it focuses on visible, transparent goals rather than on shady, questionable ones. You want to put others in a position where people can see how their behavior conforms with the organization's values.

Your values cannot be just words and ideas. They must be part of the tangible value in your product. Your enterprise must be proud of the value it puts in its products, services, and standards. Your customers must be proud of the value they get from those products. If you use people's pride correctly, you will always beat the competition. Sometimes you must defend a higher price. Focus on the better value embodied in your product. You always want to offer the best value for the money.

Honesty and directness will always lend an advantage to your ventures. Your market strength is built on trust and dependability.

Remember:

- ⊠ Your mission and values are your key to differentiation.
- ⊠ Make people proud of doing business with you.

6. Know When to Pause

What do I do when making progress becomes temporarily too difficult?

Strategy teaches that you take what is given to you. You don't try to force things to happen. In this situation, it is the pause that refreshes.

You must stabilize your position when your new venture or your market is in turmoil. You always want to advance your position, but you have to wait until certain changes in your marketplace quiet down.

All enterprises have temporary limits that restrict what they can do to meet their goals. There are resource limitations. There are information limitations. There are legal limitations. There are span-of-control limitations.

You do not test these limitations. Leave yourself plenty of room for error. Give your ventures a margin of safety. You want to force your competitors to their limits. You must know and respect your own limitations. Your competitors can ignore their limitations. There is no need for you to make the same mistake.

Making great progress takes you into unknown areas. You don't want progress to trip you up. Problems can hide in the shadows of your business. A successful fashion can quickly become a worn-out fad. Your success can lead to confusion. You may not see that you are going against the changing trends. The confusion of markets can always surprise you. You must pause to reanalyze your market position. You never want to be surprised.

Progress demands continual analysis, information, and observation.

When your resources are stretched to the limit, you must hire more people. During these periods, you must not challenge your competitors. You must organize your operations. You must train your people to meet the competition. You must build up your resources and be patient. You must do as little as possible. Make the minimum adjustments necessary to keep up with your competitors' movements.

You must increase the size of your organization over time. To grow, you need to hold onto your current employees and hire new ones. You can depend on new, untrained employees if you tell them exactly what to do. Otherwise, they will get confused. If they are confused, they cannot be productive. You use a different approach to keep experienced, proven employees. You must let them see for themselves what needs to be done. If you micromanage them, they will go elsewhere.

You must lead your employees by inspiring them. You unite them by making them successful. They will believe in you if your predictions come true. Make it easy for employees to follow directions. Make your goals clear. They will then do what they must. If your goals are difficult to understand, you will not be able to train your people. They will make mistakes. Make your procedures easy to understand. You must understand how groups of people work.

Remember:

⊗ When your resources run thin, you must pause.

⊗ Focus on building resources before moving forward.

Final Thoughts on Undercutting Uncertainty

⊖ Competition is uncertain. It brings you into one situation after another. You must know the nine common competitive situations and how to respond to them. People will follow you and competitors will fear you if you always know what to do.

⊖ You learn the nature of markets as you explore them. You can always outmaneuver your competitors if you know how to deal with market conditions better than they do.

⊖ You use pauses to regroup, reorganize, and grow your enterprise. Don't start stumbling after making progress. Don't let your resources get stretched too thin. You can use temporary limitations to build up your position by building resources.

Learn More About This Formula

This chapter is an condensed version of the sixth volume of a nine-volume work on strategy called Sun Tzu's Playbook. *The articles in this volume are listed below.*

6.0 Situation Response: Sun Tzu's eight keys to selecting the actions most appropriate to a situation.

6.1 Situation Recognition: Sun Tzu's seven keys to situation recognition in making advances.

6.1.1 Conditioned Reflexes: Sun Tzu's four keys to knowing how we develop automatic, instantaneous responses.

6.1.2 Prioritizing Conditions: Sun Tzu's six keys to parsing complex competitive conditions into simple responses.

6.2 Campaign Evaluation: Sun Tzu's five keys to knowing how we justify continued investment in an on-going campaign.

6.2.1 Campaign Flow: Sun Tzu's six keys to seeing campaigns as a series of situations that flow logically from one to another

6.2.2 Campaign Goals: Sun Tzu's five keys to assessing the value of a campaign by a larger mission.

6.3 Campaign Patterns: Sun Tzu's seven keys to knowing how knowing campaign stages gives us insight into our situation.

6.3.1 Early-Stage Situations: Sun Tzu's six keys to understanding the common situations that arise the earliest in campaigns.

6.3.2 Middle-Stage Situations: Sun Tzu's six keys to knowing how progress creates transitional situations in campaigns.

6.3.3 Late-Stage Situations: Sun Tzu's six keys to understanding the final and most dangerous stages of campaigns.

6.4 Nine Situations: Sun Tzu's ten keys to understanding the nine common competitive situations.

6.4.1 Dissipating Situations: Sun Tzu's five keys to recognizing situations where defensive unity is destroyed.

6.4.2 Easy Situations: Sun Tzu's five keys to recognizing situations of easy initial progress.

6.4.3 Contentious Situations: Sun Tzu's four keys to identifying situations that invite conflict.

6.4.4 Open Situations: Sun Tzu's five keys to recognizing situations of that are races without a course.

6.4.5 Intersecting Situations: Sun Tzu's five keys to recognizing situations that bring people together.

6.4.6 Serious Situations: Sun Tzu's six keys to identifying situations where resources can be cut off.

6.4.7 Difficult Situations: Sun Tzu's six keys to difficult situations where serious barriers must be overcome.

6.4.8 Limited Situations: Sun Tzu's six keys to identifying situations defined by a bottleneck.

6.4.9 Desperate Situations: Sun Tzu's three keys to identifying situations where destruction is possible.

6.5 Nine Responses: Sun Tzu's twelve keys to using the best responses to the nine common competitive situations.

6.5.1 Dissipating Response: Sun Tzu's five keys to responding to dissipation by the use of offense as defense.

6.5.2 Easy Response: Sun Tzu's five keys to understanding overcoming complacency.

6.5.3 Contentious Response: Sun Tzu's five keys to responding to contentious situations by knowing how to avoid conflict.

6.5.4 Open Response: Sun Tzu's five key on keeping up with the opposition.

6.5.5 Intersecting Response: Sun Tzu's five keys to the formation of situational alliances.

6.5.6 Serious Response: Sun Tzu's six keys to responding to serious situations by finding immediate income.

6.5.7 Difficult Response: Five keys to understanding the role of persistence.

6.5.8 Limited Response: Sun Tzu's four keys to the need for secret speed in tight situations.

6.5.9 Desperate Response: Sun Tzu's five keys to knowing when to use all our resources.

6.6 Campaign Pause: Sun Tzu's five keys to knowing when to stop advancing a position.

6.7 Tailoring to Conditions: Seven keys to understanding overcoming opposition using conditions in the environment.

6.7.1 Form Adjustments: Sun Tzu's five keys to adapting our responses based on the form of the ground.

6.7.2 Size Adjustments Sun Tzu's seven keys to understanding adapting responses based on the relative size of opposing forces.

6.7.3 Strength Adjustments   Sun Tzu's nine keys to knowing how to adapt responses based on relative strength of opposing missions.

6.8 Competitive Psychology   Sun Tzu's nine keys to improving competitive psychology even in adversity and failure.

6.8.1 Adversity and Creativity   Sun Tzu's nine keys to how we use adversity to spark our creativity.

6.8.2 Strength in Adversity   Sun Tzu's seven keys to using adversity to increase a group's unity and focus.

6.8.3 Individual Toughness   Sun Tzu's eight keys to knowing how failure develops character.

—FORMULA 7—
LEVERAGE
LEAPS

Create Momentum for Dominance

Adjusting to changing conditions advances a campaign only so far. In the end, you need to gain the upper hand to create a dominating position. The campaign first works to provide a consistent product to meet the opportunity in a chaotic market. This consistency alone only takes you so far. To create a truly dominating position, you need to leap out of the market and leap over your competition. This isn't as hard as it sounds.

The science of strategy offers a simple formula for leveraging easy innovations into dominating positions. The Leverage Leaps Formula is designed to create competitive momentum. *Momentum* combines what the market expects with what it doesn't expect. Momentum comes from setting up pleasant surprises and timing those surprises to win customers.

The Chaos of the Marketplace

If I am continually adapting my business to changing circumstances, how do I create momentum for my enterprise?

Competition is not neat and tidy. We all want to work through a neat to-do list when sitting at our desk in the little protected environment of our enterprise. This isn't how success works.

Success comes from momentum. Momentum comes from balancing two opposite forces—organization and innovation—against one another.

Customers are confused by the chaos and confusion in the marketplace. Customers cannot know what they want because they do not know what they can get. This confusion requires you to be organized. You must create orderly procedures and systems. All businesses must create islands of order amid the competitive chaos. Buyer uncertainty is thereby turned into confidence. Satisfying customers' expectations gives you credibility in the marketplace.

However, there is a limit to what you can gain this way.

Predictability is boring. People like visiting islands of order, but people don't like being confined to islands of order. Eventually they grow tired of the islands they know and stop visiting them. This is what creates new opportunities. People crave new experiences, but, at the same time, they fear the unknown. People appreciate high standards, but standards are eventually taken for granted. The world is changing so fast because people always want more and are always looking for new experiences.

Well-run businesses are not necessarily successful businesses. Successful businesses need something more to establish dominance over their competition.

The Leverage Leaps Formula

INGREDIENTS:

1) Quality standards, 2) customer expectations, 3) the components of prod-ucts or processes, 4) momentum, 5) the chaos of competition

INSTRUCTIONS:

1) Organize your business with clear standards. 2) Create expecta-tions before offering any surprises. 3) Rearrange proven compo-nents of a product or process into something new and different. 4) Create momentum by shifting suddenly to something unexpected. 5) Time your shift to the unexpected for maximum advantage.

Remember:
- ❂ Marketplaces are chaotic.
- ❂ You must leverage the chaos of the marketplace
- ❂ You leverage chaos by creating momentum.

1. Establish Standards to Create Order

How can I make my business easy for customers to appreci-ate?

You must understand how customers experience your business. They are always comparing you to your competitors. You must organize what is confusing. When they visit your island of order in the confusing sea of the marketplace, they must know what to expect. To create a satisfying experience, you need to establish QUALITY STANDARDS. You must use systems that have proven to be dependable.

Once they know you, customers want consistency. They need predictability. You can't help that the marketplace is chaotic, but you can eliminate any uncertainty within your operations. You cre-ate customer expectations and must know how to satisfy them.

You cannot make money without standard procedures. Chaos isn't profitable. It wastes time, effort, and resources. Organizing saves time, effort, and resources. This is where planning works. You perfect systems, practice procedures, train people, eliminate mistakes, and tighten up operations.

Good businesses organize to make money. Great businesses organize to better satisfy customers while making money. You cannot undermine the customer experience. Customers must understand the basics of what you offer. Make it easy for customers to buy. They don't want to work. You must provide consistency quickly, with a minimum of effort.

Remember:

- ⊗ Marketplaces are chaotic.
- ⊗ You organize to give customers predictability.
- ⊗ You organize to save money and create happy customers.

2. Create Realistic Expectations

Don't I have to be different to get attention in the crowded marketplace?

You cannot base your enterprise on being different. You establish quality standards to set CUSTOMER EXPECTATIONS. You then use surprise to win them over. When you use surprise at the wrong time, customers see you as a nut. Nuts get attention, but they don't win customers. People cross the street to avoid a nut because nuts are just too unpredictable.

Before you can surprise people, they need expectations about who you are and what you offer. They must know that you aren't just a nut. Even in crowded competitive conditions, it is a mistaken to think that you first have to get people's attention.

The business context can teach people to expect "a surprise." For example, if you are watching the Super Bowl, a crazy commercial cannot surprise you. Everyone expects loony commercials during the Super Bowl, and everyone also know that those commercials cost millions. They aren't really nuts.

You can only be different when people already know what you are being different from.

Of course, because you are expecting it, a crazy Super Bowl commercial isn't a surprise either.

For a surprise to work, the context has to frame your position correctly. When I give a keynote speech on strategy at a convention, I always start my presentation with something that the audience doesn't expect. Surprise works because their expectations have already been set. They know I am not a nut because the organization is paying several thousand dollars for me to talk to them.

An innovation cannot create a dominant position unless it is built on a solid foundation. Standards come first. The latest new electronic gadget is designed according to set standards, made mostly of proven components, built in factories by systems, and marketed and distributed by well-established procedures. For something "new" to work, it has to have a lot of old in it.

People can't relate to concepts that are too new. Personal computers didn't catch on until software makers realized that they needed to put more "old" into them. There were hundreds of calculating programs for personal computers before the first "electronic spreadsheet" was introduced. The fact that the electronic spreadsheet was modeled after something old, the standard accounting spreadsheet, was the key to its success, and, to a large degree, the whole success of the personal computer itself.

The simplest application of the Leverage Leaps Formula is to combine old and new product ideas together into a single package. The old idea part of the formula provides the context. This is a standard that people can understand. It creates their expectations. The new part is the surprise. It gets their attention and stimulates them with something new.

Remember:

- Without expectations, surprise is just nutty.
- When framed by expectations, surprise gets attention.
- If you leverage expectations, surprise does more than just get attention.

3. Rearrange Existing Components

How can I always come up with new ideas to create surprise and innovation?

Strategy puts a big burden on creativity. You must plan some type of innovation every time you start a new venture. You use the nature of your opportunity, your market space, and the stage of the campaign to guide your choice of innovations. If you don't use surprise and innovation, your competitors will. Innovation harnesses the flow of change in the business environment to your benefit.

Where do you get these creative ideas? As always, today's problems are the seeds for tomorrow's inspiration. You always use your time to think of ways to improve your products and systems. If you think about the COMPONENTS OF PRODUCTS AND PROCESSES, you will come up with new ways to arrange them to create surprise and momentum.

Rearranging parts is the key. Just think about what the parts are, how they can be rearranged, and the implications of making changes. You just break everything down into its components and rearrange those components. In sales and marketing, there are only a few basic messages for selling products. In manufacturing, there are only a few key components to any product. In operations, there are only a few basic steps in any business processes. Just mix them up in your mind and see what happens.

What was the process of buying a cup of coffee before the half decaf, low fat venti mocha latte? How did Starbucks change it to create a dominant position? Coffee was one size fits all, but Starbucks added a million options. Now, you give your order to a clerk. The clerk writes it on a cup, repeats it the way you *should* have said it, and passes it to the coffee maker—barrista, if you prefer. I find this process annoying because, when the clerk repeats the order, I feel like I am being corrected for not using the official coffee terminology and proper word order.

How could you reinvent the process that Starbucks reinvented? Just rearrange things a little. Let your customers grab the size of cup they want, check off the little boxes themselves, and pass it to the coffee person. Voilà! No need to worry about terminology! No corrections! No mistakes!

You may not think you are creative, but you can always just rearrange things. Rearrange messages for marketing. Rearrange parts for new products. Rearrange steps for new processes. Just by rearranging, you come up with a new perspective. Do your customers usually pay at the end of the process? How could they pay at the beginning? Starbucks moved paying to the middle.

Not all new ideas will work at first, but you can learn from your mistakes. It takes time to get innovations working. Frequently, the reason your innovation didn't work is that you didn't include enough "old" in your formula. Standards come first. Proven ideas that meet people's expectations are always the major ingredient. Innovation and proven practices are mutually dependent on each other. Standards inspire creativity, which inspires new standards. Using both, you can continually improve your business.

Without first establishing a baseline of standards, innovation and surprise are just chaos and confusion. Without innovation, standards are boring and just fall behind a marketplace that is constantly moving forward. You must combine standards with surprises to make the leap into a dominant position.

Remember:

- ⊠ There are limitless possibilities for innovation.
- ⊠ New inventions are just old ideas with a dash of difference.
- ⊠ Just rearrange the components in things and see what you get.

4. Create Momentum Shifting to Something New

How can I use innovation to get a competitive advantage?

All enterprises have both strengths and weaknesses. Weaknesses create strengths and strengths create weaknesses. Standards create the possibility of innovation, and innovation leads to new standards. Once you establish and satisfy a set of expectations, you can innovate. This innovation creates surprise.

It is the addition of surprise to a solid position that creates the MOMENTUM toward a dominant position. Momentum never comes from consistency alone. The sense of momentum is created by a surprise—changes that get attention.

To offer a sports analogy, a team that is expected to win doesn't develop any momentum by scoring. Everyone expects the dominant team to score. Everyone expects the dominant team to be ahead in the game. When is momentum created? When something surprising happens in the game. This momentum is psychological

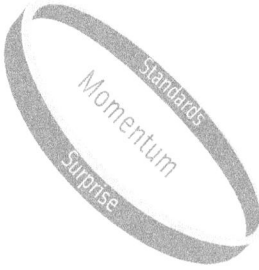

and real. When expectations are exceeded, abilities are enhanced. When expectations are disappointed, abilities decline. A surprise opens up entirely new possibilities.

How many times have we witnessed this in sports? The underdog scores and momentum changes. Suddenly the favorite can't do anything right and the underdog can't make a mistake. Unless something else surprising happens, momentum doesn't change. The favorite can score, but momentum is still against them. They have to score in a surprising way, doing something that they don't normally do, for momentum to shift again.

You cannot control the chaos of the business environment. You can, however, control your momentum. You can do something surprising to change the situation. The change puts your competitors on the defensive. When you get momentum on your side, your competitors have to copy you. You can move from one innovation to another, abandoning them when they are no longer surprising. You can keep opponents following behind you. You don't have to worry as much about competitors when competitors are worrying about you. Your momentum with customers forces competitors to keep up.

Remember:

- ✖ You use surprise to create a sense of market momentum.
- ✖ Surprise gives you control over a chaotic situation.
- ✖ Just rearrange the components in things and see what you get.

5. Time Innovation for Maximum Advantage

When do I introduce an innovation?

Together, the shift between standards and surprise creates momentum toward a dominant position, but timing is critical in securing that position. THE CHAOS OF COMPETITION is your target. You want changes to have an impact on the market. You can defuse the power of innovation by releasing changes at the wrong time or in the wrong way. Bundle small changes together to give them weight. Save up changes to release them to leverage.

Constant hidden innovation in the business builds up pressure. Timing reveals those surprises, releasing that pressure at the right time. Timing introduces a critical amount of control into the chaos of battle. It is this control that does the most to affect competitive attitudes.

You cannot release changes too soon, but you also cannot go too long without making changes. One step should follow another quickly. This type of continual progress can wash away any obstacles in a business and frustrate your competitors. This is the power of momentum.

Time surprises to impact customers. Customers' decisions take place in an instant. You must make an impact to win their business. Prepare your surprises for customers in advance but keep them a secret. Release them at the right time to get the customer decision that you want. This requires timing.

You must invest only in efforts that win customers. The shift from standards to surprise must have an impact. You must time your surprises precisely. A change from what is expected creates tension. You must time your surprise to create excitement among customers.

From customers' viewpoints, the excitement of change gives them the emotional impetus to make a decision. From the competitors' viewpoint, releasing an innovation at the right time increases their confusion and decreases their confidence. Even a small change from expectations can be enough to tip the balance if it is introduced at the right time.

The change must be intro- duced at just the right time to catch everyone off guard.

The world of competition is chaotic and confusing. You create expectations to give people the sense that they are in control. You create pleasant surprises to stimulate customers and to control them. These same surprises give your opponents the sense that you are in control. Since you and your people are more prepared for the change than customers and competitors are, you do attain more control the over chaos of the market than your competitors do.

If competitors have a sense that you are in control, you have secured a dominant position. If they panic, they will make mistakes. These mistakes create new opportunities to advance.

You create a dominant position for momentum. You do not create it by asking yourself or your people to work harder. You must innovate the ways you handle the customer experience. You shape customers' expectations to move them. Customers move forward when they know what to expect. Make customers comfortable and they will stay with you. You use surprise to challenge them to act in a new way. Give customers a sense of belonging and they will stay with you. Bring customers together and they will move forward.

You use momentum to control customers. You use customers to control competitors. You want to shape the process so both customers and competitors rush forward without stopping.

Remember:

- You control the competition by controlling customers.
- You control customers by timing your surprises correctly.
- Changing momentum can panic your competitors into making mistakes.

Final Thoughts on Leveraging Leaps

-⊖- Give people a refuge from the chaotic world by using standards that produce a consistent product. Start by giving people clear expectations about what they will get from dealing with you and satisfy those expectations.

-⊖- People get bored with having their expectations met. Give them something new and exciting in the way that you do business. They will keep coming back for more.

-⊖- Time your surprises to win over customers. Force your competitors to continually play catch-up. Give your competitors the sense that you are in control of a chaotic market. They will continually feel at a disadvantage. This will pressure them into making mistakes. Their mistakes will open new opportunities for you.

Learn More About This Formula

This chapter is an condensed version of the seventh volume of a nine-volume work on strategy called Sun Tzu's Playbook. *The articles in this volume are listed below.*

7.0 Creating Momentum: Sun Tzu's seven keys to knowing how momentum requires creativity.

7.1 Order from Chaos: Sun Tzu's seven keys to seeing the value of chaos in creating competitive momentum.

7.1.1 Creating Surprise: Sun Tzu's five keys to creating surprise using our chaotic environment.

7.1.2 Momentum Psychology: Sun Tzu's five keys to the psychology of surprise.

7.1.3 Standards and Innovation: Sun Tzu's seven keys to the methodology of creativity.

7.2 Standards First: Sun Tzu's seven keys to the role of standards in creating connections with others.

7.2.1 Proven Methods: Sun Tzu's eight keys to identifying and recognizing the limits of best practices.

7.2.2 Preparing Expectations: Sun Tzu's eight keys to knowing how we shape other people's expectation.

7.3 Strategic Innovation: Sun Tzu's six keys to understanding a simple system for innovation.

7.3.1 Expected Elements: Sun Tzu's seven keys to dividing processes and systems into components.

7.3.2 Elemental Rearrangement: Sun Tzu's six keys to seeing invention as rearranging proven elements.

7.3.3 Creative Innovation: Sun Tzu's seven keys to the more advanced methods for innovation

7.4 Competitive Timing: Sun Tzu's six keys to the role of timing in creating momentum.

7.4.1 Timing Methods: Sun Tzu's four keys to the three simplest methods of controlling timing.

7.4.2 Momentum Timing: Sun Tzu's five keys to the relative value of momentum at various times in a campaign.

7.4.3 Interrupting Patterns: Six keys to understanding how repetition creates patterns for surprise.

7.5 Momentum Limitations: Sun Tzu's six keys to the implications of momentum's temporary nature.

7.5.1 Momentum Conversion: Sun Tzu's six keys to converting momentum into positions with more value.

7.5.2 The Spread of Innovation: Sun Tzu's four keys to using the spread of innovation to advance our position.

7.6 Productive Competition: Sun Tzu's eight keys to using momentum to produce more resources.

7.6.1 Resource Discovery: Sun Tzu's six keys to using innovation to create value from seemingly worthless resources.

7.6.2 Ground Creation: Sun Tzu's six keys to understanding how we use the creation of new competitive ground to be successful.

—FORMULA 8—
ACQUIRE AWARDS

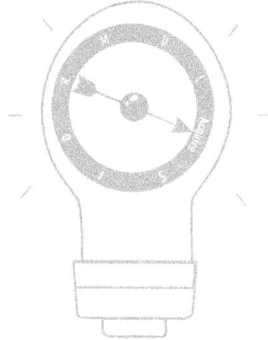

Make Victory Pay

Momentum creates a dominating position. From that position, you should attract and win customers. The operative word is "should." Every advance is an experiment. The experiment proves itself in sales. In science, you collect data to test whether your hypothesis was correct. In business, you prove your competitive positioning is correct by making sales.

The seven previous formulas put you in the position to win customers. Now you must prove that the position works to make money. This is the purpose of the Acquire Awards Formula. It isn't precisely a sales formula. Call it a customer contact formula. It eliminates unnecessary barriers that destroy sales. It add a few necessary ingredients to complete the sales link to customers.

Positioning for the Payoff

Isn't making a sale like winning a final battle with the customer?

Strategy deals with the conflict of competition. The strategic process positions you to sell the right products to the right customers. At every step, you learn more about your target market and dealing with its conditions. The knowledge you acquire is the key to helping customers buy. However, the process is not yet complete. Without this final formula, all your work is wasted. It isn't enough to win a dominating position. You must make that position pay.

All competitive positions must generate sales. Every success starts with a single sale. Your enterprise survives only as long as it consistently generates profitable sales. The campaign ends only when a new venture convinces your target market to invest in your products rather than your competitors' products.

Selling is the hardest, most emotional job in business. Every sale arises out of conflict. Only customers can choose whether to buy or not. They alone choose what they buy. You are at their mercy. In every sale, their desire for gain battles against their fear of loss. Though this conflict is internal, you play a role in the battle whenever you make contact with a customer.

Successful people know that a single mistake in customer contact can destroy all the good work of building a position. During customer contact, you can take sides in the battle between desire and fear, but you must always be on the customer's side first. The customer knows that you want to make the sale, but if you push for what you want, you are going to lose more sales than you win.

The core of customer contact is knowing your mission. Your mission connects you to the needs of your customers. A mission cannot be selfish. All missions are based on the Golden Rule—doing for others what you would have them do for you. Even if your values revolve around making a profit, those values connect you to the customers as long as you truly believe that happy customers are absolutely necessary for making a profit.

Money is a by-product of the customer contact. You follow the customers' lead to win them. You must stay in sync with what they are thinking and feeling during the process. When they get ahead of you, you must catch up. When you get ahead of them, you must slow down. You must know how to control the contact without seeming to be in control.

You can only insist on a decision from the customer when momentum is on your side. Insisting on a decision just because you want to close the sale is disastrous.

The Acquire Awards Formula

INGREDIENTS:

1) Prospects in your target market, 2) prepared questions about their individual desires, 3) pictures, props, and gimmicks, 4) a pinch of common sense

INSTRUCTIONS:

1) Learn what each potential customer needs. 2) Pull customers into long-term relationships instead of pushing them into a decision. 3) Use showmanship to create the right emotional response. 4) Evaluate your competitive position by how profitable sales are.

Remember:

- ⊠   Conflict is inherent in sales decisions.
- ⊠   You destroy the sale if you don't find a way around conflict.
- ⊠   The secret is to focus only on your long-term mission.

1. Learn What Specific Customers Want

Won't a superior market position automatically get customers to buy?

You position yourself in markets, that is, with groups of people. Groups do not make purchases. Only individuals do. You position yourself to contact PROSPECTS IN YOUR TARGET MARKET, but you must win the individual to get into a sale. You cannot use a good position to pressure individuals into buying. Even pressure from your knowledge and conviction does not work consistently. You cannot pressure others to see the value in what you are selling.

Every individual is different. Every sale is new. You must learn quickly what individual customers desire. You must have PRE-PARED QUESTIONS ABOUT THEIR INDIVIDUAL DESIRES. You must demonstrate that you want learn. People don't care how much you know until they know how much you care. The faster you learn what individuals need, the faster you can help them decide.

Until you know what people think, you cannot ask individuals to make a decision. You can try different arguments. You can praise your product. You can try to lure him or her into buying. Salespeople who talk rather than listen always think that they are winning the sale. In reality, customers ignore them. Only a small fraction of their information is helpful.

You can try to shortcut the customer contact process. If you do, you will hurt your sales. Without the proper information, what you say is as likely to hurt the sale as help it. Even if you are able to close sales through pressure, without happy customers your entire venture will eventually fail.

Instead, you must say only what is absolutely needed about what you are selling. You must become your customers' partner in the process. You must know your customers' needs. You must know where their problems are. You must avoid getting bogged down in trivialities. You must be knowledgeable about your product to make the sale, but the real challenge is connecting with your customers. You must take advantage of your customers' thinking.

The customer will never believe that you care about him or her personally more than you care about yourself. The customer can believe that you put your mission above making any specific sale. Customers can believe that you put long-term values above short-term gratification because we all do it every day. Your concern about a customer's individual needs signals whether or not you believe in your mission.

Remember:

- ✖ Every person is different with different needs.
- ✖ Unless you understand customer needs, you undermine your sales.
- ✖ Say as little as possible until you understand the customer.

2. Pull Customers into a Relationship

Why would customers buy from me if I don't seem to care about making the sale?

You must forget your desire to make the sale, but without losing your passion for the product. If customers think that you are pushing for the sale, they will push against the sale. You don't want them to fight you. If customers don't fight, you make progress more easily. You can show your passion for the product. You can uncover their problems, understand their needs, and leverage the situation. You can show your enthusiasm for having them as customers.

To get a decision, you must pay attention to the customer. You must share your mission with the customer. You must be forthright and determined. You must stand up for your belief in the product. You must suggest a good process for making a decision. You must also be quiet and patient. You must keep your personal goals to yourself and let the customer dictate the pace of the process.

If serving your mission is the basis of working with customers, you can avoid the most common mistakes in customer contact. Short-term thinking exaggerates the conflicts inherent in contact. Long-term thinking allows you to find ways around objections. Your opportunities come from viewing problems through the eyes of the customer.

> *Value is only created when people pay for it. Helping people decide is the final step in creating value.*

You must also be brave enough to ask for the sale when the time is right. In the end, customers need your help to make a decision. This is how you serve them. If you don't make it clear that they have to decide, they won't decide. You leverage the situation by giving them a good reason to decide now.

Your job is to get them excited enough so that deciding is easy. You can approach different customers from different directions.

Open-minded customers like to hear a variety of reasons to buy. Get them to agree with any of a list of reasons. Then you can ask them to decide.

For narrow-minded customers, you need to find a new reason to buy. The customers haven't thought of this reason before. Dangle a surprise in front of them like bait on a hook. Ask them to decide based upon seeing the decision from a new angle. This is how you are successful in contact with narrow-minded customers.

Remember:

- ⊗ Making sales is a test of your character.
- ⊗ The first test is your ability to understand others.
- ⊗ The final test is having the courage to ask for a decision.

3. Use Showmanship

How can I get my customers to feel what I feel about my product?

You talk as little as possible until you understand your customer's needs. Then, words alone are not enough to get others to see your point. You need PICTURES, PROPS, AND GIMMICKS.

Demonstrating a product is not nearly enough. Use illustrations and charts. Use showmanship and magic.

All businesses are entertainment. If you bore customers, you cannot score sales.

Use your product knowledge to entertain and surprise them. You must develop pictures, props, and gimmicks to get people's attention. Make sure customers have the time for you to go through your routine.

Customers need a point to focus on. Tie your presentation together. Each idea must lead back to a central point of their needs. Don't offer novel concepts alone. Tie them together with comfortable, familiar ideas. Every reason to buy must amplify a single, clear message about your central mission.

When your enterprise and product are unknown, you must excite curiosity and interest. If your enterprise and product are better known, you still must keep your presentation entertaining.

You must describe a product so everyone can understand and appreciate it. You must offer a presentation that the customers will enjoy listening to. The work you put into your presentation illustrates your desire to give something valuable to customers.

You must get your customers' attention. During customer contact, you must use emotion. People only buy because they feel like buying. The purpose of showmanship is to stimulate their feelings.

Good showmanship demands an understanding of good timing. In the morning, customers have a lot on their minds. Their resistance to new information is high. During the day, their resistance fades. By evening, customers want to be entertained.

Customers are easily confused. Keep your presentations organized so that they don't frustrate listeners. If customers get nervous or frustrated, you must stay quiet while they blow off steam. Make sure that you really understand what their needs and concerns are. This is how you make customers comfortable.

When you ask for a decision, wait for your customers to respond. Stay friendly no matter what their answer. Customers must offer objections to test the strength of your beliefs. Friendliness, enthusiasm, and patience wear down the customer's resistance. You will be successful if you serve the needs of others. This is how you master persuasion.

Remember:
- Communicate your enthusiasm though showmanship.
- Think of a presentation as a form of entertainment.
- Know how to channel customers' emotions.

4. Gauge Position by Profit

How can I make sure that my venture is profitable?

Everything you have done in the Progress Cycle thus far can put you in a strong position. If you avoid some simple mistakes in customer contact, that position can be proven through sales.

First, avoid long drawn-out sales processes. Like every other part of the campaign, your first sales should be quick, small, and local. As customers are established, you can build up to larger sales and longer sales cycles. First, you must prove that your competitive position creates value for customers by generating income.

If the initial process is easy and quick and creates happy customers, your new position will be profitable. Happy customers lead to more happy customers and even more quicker, easier, and more profitable sales. Start fast to get strong. Take advantage of people's desire to follow others and build on your success.

Sales are necessary for profit, but sales alone are not enough to make victory pay.

If you generate profits quickly from new markets, those profits can quickly pay for the next round of growth and expansion.

Sales arise naturally from good positions if you do nothing to undermine them. Use common sense and do not do anything to create conscious resistance. Do not say anything to threaten firmly held beliefs. Reflect the customers' interests in everything you do.

To make ventures profitable, you must have at least A PINCH OF COMMON SENSE. Do not position your product against the market trends. Do not offer a product based on a lack of alternatives. Question customers who only pretend to agree. Do not position against your strongest competition. Do not believe everything the customer tells you.

Your only goal must be successful customer contacts, not to prove yourself and your product right. Do not continue to sell to a customer who has agreed to buy. Do not offer price discounts if they undermine your credibility or the value of your product.

If your policies create obstacles, give the customer an agreeable alternative. Do not press the customer too hard for a decision. You must use timing. Avoid asking for attention and decisions when people's minds are busy. Ask for a decision when resistance fades and customers want a resolution so that they can relax and move on. These are the simple rules of customer contact.

Customer contact is the final part of your strategy. If you have understood your strengths and weaknesses, chosen the right opportunities, and positioned your enterprise correctly, you are ready to make contact with customers. You must handle customer contact with concern for individuals and a focus on your mission. If you think long-term and use showmanship, your sales are assured.

Remember:

- Focus on customer knowledge.
- Leverage your market position.
- Don't make any stupid mistakes.

Final Thoughts on Acquiring Awards

-⊙- Your goal is to eliminate conflict from the sales process. You must take a long-term perspective in making sales while making sales as quickly as possible. Your ability to make quick sales depends on learning about each specific customer's needs.

-⊙- Selling is an emotionally demanding process. You must have the right attitude. You must understand the basics of the psychology of persuasion. You must use all the tools of communication and entertainment to make the process emotionally satisfying for your customers.

Learn More About This Formula

This chapter is an condensed version of the eight volume of a nine-volume work on strategy called Sun Tzu's Playbook. *The articles in this volume are listed below.*

8.0 Winning Rewards: Sun Tzu's six keys to knowing how we harvest the rewards of a new position.

8.1 Successful Positions: Sun Tzu's four keys to understanding the nature of a profitable position.

8.1.1 Transforming Resources: Sun Tzu's six keys to converting the intangible value of positions to the resources we need.

8.1.2 Reward Boundaries: Sun Tzu's six keys to understanding the limits of our control over a position and its rewards.

8.1.3 Reward Timing: Sun Tzu's six keys to identifying rewarding positions based upon timing.

8.2 Making Claims: Sun Tzu's five keys to claiming rewards after winning positions.

8.3 Securing Rewards: Sun Tzu's five keys to maximizing the rewards from a position.

8.3.1 Gauging Value: Sun Tzu's five keys to the methods for correctly measuring a position's value.

8.3.2 Distinctive Packaging: Sun Tzu's nine keys to creating the perception of value.

8.3.3 Rules of Engagement: Sun Tzu's nine keys outlining the do's and don't of making claims.

8.3.4 Position Production: Sun Tzu's seven keys to understanding the shift from profitable competition to profitable production.

8.4 Individual Support: Sun Tzu's eight keys to understanding the general techniques for winning the support of individuals.

8.5 Leveraging Emotions: Sun Tzu's eight keys to understanding how we use emotion to obtain rewards.

8.6 Winning Attention: Sun Tzu's eight keys to understanding how to win the attention of others for our claims.

8.7 Productivity Improvement: Sun Tzu's seven keys to improving internal production to support external competition.

8.7.1 Evaluating Erosion: Sun Tzu's eight keys to gauging the erosion of our current positions.

8.7.2 Abandoning Positions: Sun Tzu's six keys to understanding how we abandon a losing position safely.

—FORMULA 9—

SECURE SAFETY

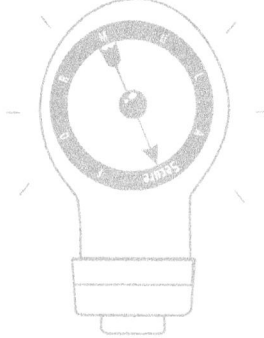

Defend From Competitive Attack

After you have proven that a competitive position pays, you need to defend that position from attack. Until you secure its safety, you have not advanced your position. New positions are fragile. Competitors are quick to copy successes. The easiest way for them to copy your success is to steal from it. You must protect the key resources on which your new position depends.

This is the final step in the Progress Cycle. The Secure Safety Formula protects your new position. It teaches you to recognize when you are vulnerable. It teaches you to prepare for the most common forms of attack. When you have a dominant position, you cannot leave openings through which opponents can undermine you. Most attacks are harmless if you respond appropriately, and that is why you must master this final formula.

SECURE

Success Is Always a Target

After I prove that my idea is financially viable, what is the most likely threat that I will face?

You must defend your new, proven position against competitors. Success invites competition. Success invites attack. Success invites imitation. Defense is the final skill you must learn.

Your success is its own reward. It is easier to defend an established position than it is to build it. As long as you don't take your new position for granted, the techniques of defending a position are relatively easy. Defense is easier and more certain than advance.

Your first line of defense is pursuing opportunities that are easy to defend (FORMULA 4). Your second line of defense is responding to competitive situations correctly (FORMULA 6). The final line of defense is protecting yourself from direct competitive attacks.

The Secure Safety Formula

INGREDIENTS:

1) Your people, 2) your suppliers., 3) your product ideas., 4) your locations, 5) your customers., 6) the support of your people, 7) the direct attack. 8) indirect attack, 9) the attack on imperfection, 10) attack to win your partners, 11) a market trends attack , 12) a cool head.

INSTRUCTIONS:

1) Defend the five targets of attack from theft and imitation. 2) Keep your people from being pulled away by competitors by leading and motivating them. 3) Respond correctly to the five most common forms of attack to easily defeat them. 4) Avoid emotional overreactions by seeing the big picture.

Remember:

- ⊗   When you find success, you will be attacked.
- ⊗   It is easier to defend a position than build it.
- ⊗   You must know the techniques for defense.

1. Defend the Five Targets

What is the most successful way for competitors to attack a new venture that is proving profitable?

The first thing you must do is to secure your position against imitators. Imitation may be the sincerest form of flattery, but it is also the easiest way for competitors to attack your position. You target opportunities that are difficult for competitors to imitate. Your position allows you to do things that they cannot. However, competitors will try to overcome this obstacle by stealing from you.

There are five ways that competitors will try to steal from you.

First, they will try to hire YOUR PEOPLE.

Second, they will try to partner with YOUR SUPPLIERS.

Third, they will try to duplicate YOUR PRODUCT IDEAS.

Fourth, they will try to undermine YOUR LOCATIONS.

Finally, they will try to contact YOUR CUSTOMERS.

You have to defend all five targets. For these attacks to succeed, you must leave an opening. If you fill the opening opponents target, you can block their duplication of the work you have pioneered.

You defend against larger competitors by using your speed.

It takes time for them to duplicate what you have done. You must be standing still for them to catch you. Large companies have the resources to duplicate your efforts, but they cannot move as quickly as you can. Your first defense is to stay ahead of them.

SECURE

The environment must make their copying your products profitable. When a market is hot, you cannot satisfy its demands completely. This invites competitors who can offer alternatives. Do not invest in marketing to stimulate desires you cannot satisfy.

You also need to keep an eye on your suppliers' market. If their industry slows down, the price of their product will drop and its availability increase. This lowers the entry costs for your competitors. You must lower your prices first.

You can know when you are susceptible to imitators by studying the signs in your environment. You must act to cut off them off before they get started. If you do nothing, you make imitation profitable.

Remember:

- ❋ Competitors will copy what you have done.
- ❋ There are five ways that they will try to steal from you.
- ❋ You can always cut them off by acting quickly.

2. Keep Your People

What is the most important element in meeting a competitive challenge?

Your people are the key to meeting challenges from the competition. You must make it difficult for competitors to steal your people. This is the quickest way for competitors to undermine your success. The easiest way to defeat this threat is to use your people well.

You must WIN THE SUPPORT OF YOUR PEOPLE. Do not overburden them. People stay where they are unless given a reason to leave. If you care about your employees and keep the workplace enjoyable, they will want to stay with you if they possibly can.

Even if you are a one-person business, these rules apply to everyone with whom you work.

Keep your employees busy and keep their jobs interesting. You don't want anyone to leave you because their skills are not utilized. If people have challenging work to do, they will not get bored. If they can advance without finding another employer, they will stay with you. Treat the people with whom you work like a family. Your people must see that you are committed to your customers. People judge how you will treat them by how they see you treat others.

Share your enterprise's success with your people. They must feel that they are being rewarded as part of the team. The more transparent you can make your enterprise's rewards, the happier people will be. If people are in the dark about rewards, they will imagine that they are being left out.

When people are dependent on your business, they lose their fear. Your people should feel that competitors are threatening them personally. Your people will then defend the enterprise without abandoning it.

Involve and educate your people. Without being told, everyone must know what to do. Without being asked, everyone must see what needed. This means they should understand these principles of strategy as well as you do. (*Subliminal message: You need to get everyone a copy of this book right now.*) If they understand their situation, they will put in their best efforts. Without being monitored, everyone will prove that they can be trusted.

People get nervous when facing competition. Your experienced people must know how to meet a competitive challenge. Stop any second-guessing by making your decisions clear. Avoid failure by leaving your people no excuses for failing. Your employees may not be rich, but this is not because they do not want to become wealthy.

People must respect your expertise as a leader. This requires confidence and detachment. You must care about your people, but you must keep your distance. Distance may not make the heart grow fonder, but it blurs your weaknesses. If you want to maintain your leadership and promote your mission, others must see you as a little more than human.

As a leader, you can never be just "one of the folks." Leadership only works if you set yourself apart.

You must control what your people see and hear. They must believe in you without your explaining your reasoning. You can reinvent people's jobs. You must be able change the enterprise's direction. Your people must follow you without questioning your decisions.

Remember:

- ⊗ The key is using your people.
- ⊗ You must keep your experienced people.
- ⊗ Your people must know what a challenge means.

3. Respond to Five Forms of Attack

How else will competitors try to attack my position besides copying me?

Everyone tries to think competitively. You must prepare for five different types of competitive challenges. You must know how to adapt to them to secure your market space.

First, competitors will try a DIRECT ATTACK. They will look for holes in the value that you bring to the market space. They will target your most marginal customers. You must defend customers who get the least benefit by bringing them closer to your enterprise.

Second, competitors will an INDIRECT ATTACK, charging you with acting in bad faith. They may launch this attack through the media or through the court system. You must remain calm in the face of these charges. They are not believable if you don't overreact.

Third, competitors will try an ATTACK ON IMPERFECTION. They will try to win away customers who are unhappy because of your inevitable mistakes. If you deal with mistakes and make things right with customers, competitors cannot use them against you.

Fourth, competitors will try an ATTACK TO WIN YOUR PART-NERS. This approach takes time. When you hear about competitors talking with your suppliers and other partners in the industry, you must concentrate on shoring up your alliances.

Finally, your competitors will try a MARKET TRENDS AT-TACK, using climate change against you. You must continually adapt to market trends. Make inexpensive changes to address short-term trends. You must invest more to address long-term trends.

You must recognize these five forms of competitive attack. You must actively protect your enterprise against them. You must respond to them immediately. If you are slow to respond, they can destroy your enterprise.

Competitive attacks are more dangerous than normal changes in the business climate. Changes in the business climate can undermine your enterprise. Changes in the climate can force you to change the way you do business. Competitive attacks are different. Competitors actively work to steal away your customers and your income. You need customers and income. Change can weaken you. Competitive attacks can destroy you.

SECURE

Remember:
- There are five forms of competitive attack.
- You can defend against them if know what to do.
- You must confront these attacks quickly and directly.

4. Do Not Overreact

How can I teach my opponents a lesson when they attack me so they won't do it again?

You must maintain a COOL HEAD. You must not overreact to competitive attacks. Don't take those attacks personally. Avoid letting them become an emotional issue. Your feelings about your competitors must not confuse you. Stay focused on your business.

You must respond to the situation, not to the emotion. You must defend your position, not hurt your competitors. In the long run, you beat the competition by finding new openings to advance your position. When your position is secure, you must focus on the next opportunity. Your success demands continual progress. You want to devote your mind to improving your business, not to hurting competitors. Your best defense against competitors is utilizing every opening they give you.

This is the science of strategy. You must know how to build a position. You must go through the nine steps of analysis to make your position competitive. If an action cannot make you money, do not invest time and effort in it. If campaigning cannot be profitable, do not waste your efforts. If your enterprise is safe, do not risk your resources.

You may hate your competitors. You may have good reason to. You may want to put them out of business, but that is not the goal. Success comes from producing profits, not a destroying others.

You must never let your emotions hurt your chances for success. The well-being of your enterprise is longer lasting than emotions.

To be successful, you must not change your position simply to create problems for competitors. Make problems for competitors only when it profits you to do so. If there is no profit in hurting your competitors, you cannot afford to act against them. You can destroy your own business in fighting your opponents.

No matter how many competitors you destroy, you will always have new competitors. If you weaken your business destroying a competitor, it is just a matter of time until the next competitor destroys you. You want to hurt competitors only when it pays to do so. You want to weaken them only when that action makes you stronger in the market as a whole. You must avoid taking actions that weaken you along with your competitors.

This is difficult because people overreact to competitive chal-lenges. We want to react emotionally. The pur-pose of learning strategy is to give you a lot to think about. If you have a lot to think about, you are less likely to react emotionally.

If you want to be successful, there are many emotions that you just cannot afford.

Any attack can be a problem, but it can also be an opportunity. You must look at every attack dispassionately, seeing whether you can turn it to your advantage. For every attack that hurts you, there will be another attack that helps you. Only your com-petitors can create opportunities for you.

Remember, you don't know what the future will bring. Strategy is not a plan. Competition is chaotic. Situations that upset you today may one day make you happy. A little temporary frustration often leads to greater future pleasure. Competitors can be enemies today and friends tomorrow. The business climate is always chang-ing.

SECURE

If you destroy a competitor, you cannot bring him or her back. A worse competitor may take his or her place. Worse, the resources that the battle costs you are lost forever.

Knowing this, you must be careful. Success come from advancing your position. Success comes from defending your position. Your only mission must be to keep the position strong and to make every new venture profitable.

Remember:

- Avoid emotional reactions to competitive attacks.
- React to competitive situations, not to your emotions about your competitors.
- Focus only on advancing your position and you will see as many opportunities in attacks as problems.

Final Thoughts on Securing Safety

-⊖- Truly dominating positions make attacks extremely difficult. If you pick the right opportunities and build up the right positions, you can prevent competitors from even thinking about challenging you.

-⊖- Competitors follow the path of least resistance. If you make what you do look difficult, they will be much less likely to copy you. It is worth the time to control appearances.

-⊖- It is always easier to defend than attack. If you establish a position first, it will always be more profitable for you to defend it than it will be for competitors to attack it.

Learn More About This Formula

This chapter is an condensed version of the ninth volume of a nine-volume work on strategy called Sun Tzu's Playbook. *The articles in this volume are listed below.*

9.0 Understanding Vulnerability: Sun Tu's six keys to understanding the use of common environmental attacks.

9.1 Fire Storm Vulnerability: Sun Tzu's seven keys to understanding our vulnerability to environmental crises.

9.1.1 Climate Rivals: Sun Tzu's six keys to preparing against how changing conditions create opponents.

9.1.2 Threat Development: Sun Tzu's seven keys to knowing how changing conditions create environmental threats.

9.2 Points of Vulnerability: Sun Tzu's five keys to seeing our points of vulnerability during an environmental crisis.

9.2.1 Personnel Risk: Sun Tzu's five keys to the vulnerability of key individuals.

9.2.2 Immediate Resource Risk: Sun Tzu's five keys to the resources required for immediate use.

9.2.3 Logistics Risk: Sun Tzu's four keys to knowing how firestorms choke normal channels of movement and communication.

9.2.4 Asset Risk: Sun Tzu's four keys to understanding the threats to our fixed assets.

9.2.5 Organizational Risk: Sun Tzu's five keys to the targeting the roles and responsibilities within an organization.

9.3 Crisis Leadership: Sun Tzu's nine keys to maintaining the support of our supporters during attacks.

9.3.1 Mutual Danger: Sun Tzu's six keys to understanding how we use mutual danger to create mutual strength.

9.3.2 Message Control: Sun Tzu's five keys to communication methods to use during a crisis.

9.4 Crisis Defense: Sun Tzu's five keys to knowing how vulnerabilities are exploited and defended during a crisis.

9.4.1 Division Defense: Sun Tzu's five keys to preventing organizational division during a crisis.

9.4.2 Panic Defense: Sun Tzu's four keys to preventing mistakes from panic during a crisis.

9.4.3 Defending Openings: Sun Tzu's four keys to knowing how to defend openings created by a crisis.

9.4.4 Defending Alliances: Sun Tzu's five keys to dealing with guilt-by-association.

9.4.5 Defensive Balance: Sun Tzu's four keys to using short-term conditions to tip the balance in a crisis.

9.5 Crisis Exploitation: Sun Tzu's five keys to how to successfully use an opponent's crisis.

9.5.1 Adversarial Opportunities: Sun Tzu's eight keys to knowing how our opponents' crises can create opportunities.

9.5.2 Avoiding Emotion: Sun Tzu's six keys to the danger of exploiting environmental vulnerabilities for purely emotion reasons.

9.6 Constant Vigilance: Sun Tzu's five keys to understanding where to focus our attention to preserve our positions.

—SUMMARY—

SUCCESS
IN A NUTSHELL

Nine Final Thoughts on Strategy

1. About the 9 key components: Let your competitors be deceived by appearances. Even knowing the formula, it is psychologically difficult to take a hard, realistic look at your competitive position and admit where you fall behind your competitors, but that is where you must start if you want to surpass your competitors.

2. About finding friends: Let your competitors think that information comes from internal systems or external media. You need to find people who can broaden your thinking. This right range of contacts gives you a broad range of thinking. This is the most valuable asset in competitive strategy.

3. About observing opportunities: Let your competitors think that they have to chase every "opportunity" that comes their way. When you learn to see the emptiness around you, you recognize all the possibilities your position makes possible. The challenge is picking the right opening, where the emptiness fits your resources.

4. About recognizing restrictions: Let your opponents stake out positions that they cannot defend or that block their future progress. You are not limited by money and resources. Over time your only real restrictions come from choosing the wrong positions. Remember to use the six benchmark regions to help you know what you are getting into.

5. About minimizing mistakes: Let your competitors make the big plans and take the big risks. Even if they get lucky, you don't have to beat them because they will eventually beat themselves. You must test opportunities using the secrets of focus. If a focused advance doesn't work on a small scale, nothing will work on a larger scale.

6. About undercutting uncertainty: Let your competitors get caught unprepared for the way situations change. You can respond appropriately to the nine common competitive situations and put yourself into an advantageous position in any of the four types of marketplaces.

7. About leveraging leaps: Let your competitors make changes that don't matter. You must know how to alternate proven standards with surprise to create momentum at the right time to create a dominating position.

8. About acquiring awards: Let your rivals lose sight of the only real goal. You must know how to use a dominating position to generate sales, avoiding the pitfalls of customer contact.

9. About the securing safety: Let your competitors leave their successes open to attack. You should know how to guard the five competitive targets from the five most common types of attack.

About the Author

This book's award-winning author, Gary Gagliardi, is America's leading authority on Sun Tzu's *The Art of War.* A frequent guest on radio and television talk shows, Gary has written over twenty books on strategy. Ten of his books on Sun Tzu's methods have won award recognition

Gary Gagliardi   in business, self-help, career, sports, philosophy, multicultural, and youth nonfiction categories.

Gary began studying Sun Tzu's philosophy over thirty years ago. His understanding of strategy was proven in the business world, where his software company became one of the Inc. 500 fastest-growing companies in America and won numerous business awards. After selling his software company, Gary began writing about and teaching Sun Tzu's strategic philosophy full time.

He has spoken all over the world on a variety of topics concerning competition, from modern technology to ancient history. His books have been translated into many languages, including Japanese, Thai, Korean, Russian, Indonesian, and Spanish.

Today lives in Las Vegas with his wife, Rebecca.

gagliardi.gary@gmail.com

Want to learn more about Sun Tzu's strategy?

SunTzuS.com
Science of Strategy Institute

eBooks

Audio books

Audio seminars

Online training

Books By Gary Gagliardi

Sun Tzu's Art of War Playbook (Nine Volumes)
Sun Tzu's The Art of War Plus The Art of Sales
9 Formulas for Business Success
The Golden Key to Strategy
The Art of War Plus The Chinese Revealed
The Art of War Plus The Art of Management
Art of War Plus The Art of Marketing
The Art of War Plus The Art of Politics (with Shawn Frost)
Making Money By Speaking
The Warrior Class: 306 Lessons in Strategy
The Art of War for the Business Warrior
The Art of War Plus The Warrior's Apprentice (for teens)
The Art of War Plus Strategy for Sales Managers
The Ancient Bing-fa: Martial Arts Strategy
Strategy Against Terror: Ancient Wisdom for Today's War
The Art of War Plus The Art of Career Building
The Art of War Plus Its Amazing Secrets
The Art of War Plus The Art of Love
The Art of War Plus The Art of Parenting Teens

www.ingramcontent.com/pod-product-compliance
Lightning Source LLC
Chambersburg PA
CBHW072351200326
41519CB00015B/3733